D0061039

Exploring Everyday Life

Exploring Everyday Life

Strategies for Ethnography and Cultural Analysis

Billy Ehn, Orvar Löfgren, and Richard Wilk

ROWMAN & LITTLEFIELD
Lanham • Boulder • New York • London

Published by Rowman & Littlefield
A wholly owned subsidary of The Rowman & Littlefield Publishing Group, Inc.
4501 Forbes Boulevard, Suite 200, Lanham, Maryland 20706
www.rowman.com

Unit A, Whitacre Mews, 26-34 Stannary Street, London SE11 4AB, United Kingdom

Copyright © 2016 by Rowman & Littlefield

All rights reserved. No part of this book may be reproduced in any form or by any electronic
or mechanical means, including information storage and retrieval systems, without written
permission from the publisher, except by a reviewer who may quote passages in a review.

British Library Cataloguing in Publication Information Available

Library of Congress Cataloging-in-Publication Data

Ehn, Billy, 1946–
  Exploring everyday life : strategies for ethnography and cultural analysis / Billy Ehn, Orvar
Löfgren, and Richard Wilk.
    pages cm
  Includes bibliographical references and index.
  ISBN 978-0-7591-2405-9 (cloth : alk. paper) — ISBN 978-0-7591-2406-6 (pbk. : alk. paper)
— ISBN 978-0-7591-2407-3 (electronic) 1. Ethnology—Methodology. I. Löfgren, Orvar.
II. Wilk, Richard R. III. Title.
  GN345.E43 2015
  305.8001—dc23

                                                                                    2015014340

∞™ The paper used in this publication meets the minimum requirements of American
National Standard for Information Sciences—Permanence of Paper for Printed Library
Materials, ANSI/NISO Z39.48-1992.

Printed in the United States of America

CONTENTS

1

HIDDEN WORLDS

This is a book about exploring the mysteries of everyday life, all those seemingly trivial tasks and routines that shape people's lives, often in unconscious ways. They are activities that seem unimportant and are rapidly forgotten: a passing feeling, something caught at a glance, things hardly noticed. Whether waiting for a bus, vacuuming the apartment, or daydreaming in class, when nothing seems to be happening, a lot is actually going on. There is an invisible world at the end of your nose: objects you no longer see, words you no longer hear, tastes that are overfamiliar, tasks that have turned into mere reflexes.

Why this focus on everyday life? Isn't this a terrain that is all too familiar? On the contrary. These undercurrents in people's lives often go unnoticed, both by people caught in the daily flow of routines and by scholars trying to understand people's behavior. It is precisely because many of these mundane activities tend to be invisible—seen as unimportant or just taken for granted—that they play such a powerful role, especially in the reproduction of society. Or as the German sociologist Georg Simmel (1910) once put it: all those small details and situations work together "to make society possible."

In much cultural research, there has been a preoccupation with the explicit: the visible and dramatic. Therefore we want to turn the gaze away from such front-stage activities and move backstage. Instead of beginning with issues or statements that are constantly voiced, we argue for the use of side entrances. By starting in the everyday, it is possible to find surprising connections between small matters and large issues.

Seemingly trivial routines may hide important conflicts or carry strong moral messages. Underneath the media discussions of accelerating change or cultural flux, we can find surprising evidence for continuity. Inconspicuous activities may be gendered in ways that produce patterns of dominance, and issues of class and ethnicity turn up in surprising corners. Most important, subtle details of daily life still hold many secrets.

Our book has three main aims. First, we will demonstrate new ways of grasping what's going on in an elusive reality. We discuss a broad range of ethnographic research strategies as well as new perspectives on cultural analysis, drawing on a number of current theoretical and methodological trends.

Second, we use concrete examples to show how a study or a paper assignment can evolve step-by-step: from the first wild ideas, onto the constant dialogue between materials and analysis, through to the final writing and presentation of conclusions.

Third, we show what happens when these kinds of ethnography and cultural analysis are applied to topics that are relevant to future employment. We emphasize the development of practical skills and show how they can be deployed creatively in many different settings. The techniques for understanding everyday activities can be used in an unending spectrum of tasks and problems that students will face in their working lives.

FINDING THE TOOLS

Our methodological approach is thus ethnographic; it is about qualitative techniques for collecting or producing material on social life in different settings through interviews, observations, and other fieldwork procedures where the researcher is personally present in "the field" of study. This is an approach originally developed in social anthropology but nowadays used in many disciplines, from sociology and cultural studies to business economics and management. Our theoretical perspectives come from the interdisciplinary tradition of cultural analysis, where the focus is on shared understandings and practices.

The following chapters provide a set of tools for making the everyday visible and tangible, problematizing that which is taken for granted or just ignored as trivial. A number of hands-on techniques are demonstrated, aimed at catching both the elusive and fleeting. How does one describe actions and reactions people often find hard to verbalize?

In presenting devices for managing this task, we argue for methodological experimentation and a certain degree of analytical playfulness. What kinds of ethnographic strategies are helpful in order to be able to peek into blind spots, peer around corners, or look under the furniture? What theoretical views may help in the understanding of why some kinds of social life become perceptible, while so many others remain unseen? In the following chapters we will also show, by referring to other researchers from different disciplines, how to get inspiration and guidance.

We will use a number of case studies to provide a practical approach to how a study can be organized, materials discovered, and a paper written. Our examples are of various kinds. We show how, for example, analyzing a family meal, a daily commute, a DIY project, or a young couple moving in together

Figure 1.1.   Sometimes the most important thing might be just under your feet.
(Richard Wilk)

can reveal interesting and often surprising insights into major social questions and cultural dilemmas. These examples demonstrate that mundane rules, rituals, and attitudes are the very substance of culture. The book is thus an invitation to enter this terrain and start thinking about all the potential materials and problems one may encounter at any time. How can this territory be explored and the findings turned into a student paper, an essay, or a thesis outline?

Increasingly, students and scholars doing ethnography and cultural analysis today often work as "bricoleurs" combining very different kinds of materials and methods, and using tools such as the cell phone and the Internet. The book explores how one can start collecting and integrating all kinds of ethnographic materials for a study: YouTube videos, Facebook discussions, newspaper clippings, photo snapshots, passing remarks in a conversation, a scene from a soap opera, or a line from a song. How does one turn such a "bricolage" into a platform for analysis, and how can different materials complement or provoke one another?

The bricolage approach is also an effective way of kick-starting a paper and tackling situations when writing gets stuck or ideas don't materialize. In the world of urgent research deadlines, there is a need for practical and quick solutions. When you have just a month for producing an essay or an outline of a PhD dissertation, the advice and the examples in this book will help you.

FROM IDEA TO FINISHED PRODUCT

In many research handbooks, a well-organized work process is often presented with neat steps. In these books, a study moves systematically from finding a theme, to deciding on aim and scope, to going to the library or surfing the Net to find ideas and choose a theoretical framework. By then, it is time to collect material or go out to do some ethnography. After this, the collected material is analyzed, and finally, the study is written up.

Reality is much more chaotic. Our hands-on approach disentangles the often indirect process through which a paper or an essay is constructed. In the case studies, we highlight the various moves from the first messy search for ideas and materials to the ways that one can weave writing and analysis together and, hopefully, end up with a finished product. The successful study or the essay with surprising findings is often the result of a constant intermingling of writing, data producing, and analysis. We argue for a need to constantly shift between writing, analysis, and gathering materials. New ideas, fruitful materials, and analytical insights pop up in unexpected situations and places.

This doesn't mean that we argue for a kind of happy-go-lucky amateur approach. On the contrary, such an analytic movement back and forth calls for special research skills and careful planning, and combining an open mind with analytical rigor. Ethnography is not about just going out "looking for stuff" but requires patient training, for example, in the ability to look at situations from different perspectives.

The competences of project management, recording, analysis, and reporting are not only part of university education but also a toolbox that is valuable on the job market. Quickly grasping a problem, gathering information from different sources, and then producing a report on time—all the while, finding new approaches and unusual viewpoints—are useful talents.

THE NEED FOR A CULTURAL PERSPECTIVE

The book presents a cultural perspective on everyday life as a way to understand larger issues in society. This means that people's perceptions and habits are cultural products. They are learned, exercised, communicated, and transformed during the course of life. Those processes take place in interactions with people and objects as well as through mass media and other public events.

Figure 1.2.   Where is the field? It is not necessarily "out there somewhere" in exotic surroundings. It might even be in a familiar setting like this library. (Billy Ehn)

The learning perspective enables us to see how people—often uncon-sciously—come to understand how an ordinary situation such as a queue works, or what happens when morning routines are interrupted. We explore how habits are made and unmade as well as the many forms of absentminded multitasking. The experienced hand dives for the car keys, sets the table, or locates the soap in the shower, while the attention is directed somewhere else, into daydreaming, for example. We track the ways people learn and naturalize skills into something patently obvious. Routines sink into the body and turn into reflexes.

This approach moves away from the study of culture as narratives and texts, as something mainly verbal and intellectual, to a stronger emphasis on nonverbal cultural practices, and also on the materiality of seemingly mental activities. Many of the capacities and shared understandings that are used in everyday life, which make society work, are implicit, embodied knowledge, and are seldom reflected upon by the conscious mind.

This kind of unconsciousness is one of the most surprising things about everyday life. We don't mean that people are asleep or drugged; we mean that they do amazingly complex things without being aware of it. Every day, all of us take part in an elaborate choreography, as intricate as the plot of any novel, where, more or less unaware of it, we coordinate our actions with other people.

Humans thus spend a large amount of their time on "automatic pilot," letting their unconscious mind drive their routine actions, while their con-scious mind is free for what is regarded as "more important" stuff—talking with friends, for example, or reading books or watching TV. Usually you don't even know you have these automatic habits until they break down because someone moved the soap, changed the position of the car seat, or rearranged the shelves at the supermarket.

ANALYTICAL STRATEGIES

Our aim to describe unconscious routines calls for well-reasoned ethnographic approaches. In the following chapters we will outline a number of methods for flushing hidden habits and understandings out into the open.

One strategy is the use of a historical perspective as a way of problematiz-ing the present. This approach may start by simply describing a contemporary phenomenon in the past tense, for example, seeing Facebook as a piece of cultural history or using contrasting materials from other historical periods. What does a family meal or a morning makeup ritual stand for today, and how were they perceived earlier? The historical approach also is important when it comes to understanding how people learn new habits or ideas in ways that slowly make them self-evident. For example, we show that an ethnography of the morning commute may benefit from going back in time to see how people painstakingly tried to adopt a new form of transportation such as the train. How do you learn the skills of commuting?

Another central approach concerns the importance of materiality: the intensive interaction between people and objects or physical surroundings. Instead of getting stuck in a world overflowing with words and texts, you should also look at the constant engagement with commonplace objects such as coffee mugs, cars, clothes, and cell phones. They become extensions of one's body, willing or unwilling partners of cooperation, but also carriers of memories and meanings. Doing the "archaeology of the everyday" can help us to gain access to the secret world of things. We will discuss in detail the kinds of special ethnographic methods needed to catch these kinds of interactions.

One more rewarding and understudied dimension of everyday life is its emotional importance. Under the surface of habits, there are often strong feelings that may suddenly emerge. Disturbances in the usual procedures can generate irritation, passion, anger, acute boredom, or strong longings. There is much mental energy harnessed to judging the proper ways of carrying out morning practices, family meals, or taking out the trash. Every routine act is therefore a path to discovering the micro-politics of power, key moral judgments, and value investments. Subtle or strong emotional expressions are an alert that an ordinary practice or situation hides strong cultural issues or conflicts.

STRUCTURE OF THE BOOK

The ethnographic strategies and analytical approaches we have mentioned are discussed in a number of case studies. Each chapter concentrates on certain major methodological questions and is followed by examples of exercises that illustrate how the approach can be used in different fields of study.[1]

The next chapter after this introduction, "The Importance of Small Things," is about getting started. We illustrate how a study can be prepared and organized over a couple of days or a week. Where do you begin? How do you search for ideas and materials and begin writing from day one? The aim is to avoid an idealized textbook narrative of going from A to Z and, instead, show how any study is a journey that usually ends in a different place from what was

---

[1] The book is a joint project. However, some chapters have a single author in charge of the text. In chapters 4 and 8, "I" is Richard Wilk; in chapter 5 and 6, Orvar Löfgren; and in chapter 7, Billy Ehn.

anticipated. The case chosen is a study of what happens when a young couple moves in together for the first time, into a new apartment.

How can you begin gathering ideas for a topic like this by surfing the Net, doing quick interviews with friends, looking for potential materials and questions anywhere? What kinds of analytical questions may crop up with a theme like this? Why do small things become so important or irritating in establishing a new home? How do my good routines and your bad habits create friction and open up moral issues? What divisions of labor are cemented or contested? The chapter illustrates how different analytical and ethnographical paths may be chosen and where they can lead.

The third chapter, "Making the Familiar Strange," continues to explore the world of routines and daily rhythms, illustrating how one can focus on seemingly insignificant and invisible parts of everyday life. Cultural researchers are supposed to be able to look at familiar phenomena with "new eyes," turning the mundane into the exotic. The home is a good example of something so well known and familiar that it is a real challenge to see it in a new light. In this chapter we will use the home to develop analytical strategies to problematize what is taken for granted. What research techniques and analytical approaches are needed to get behind all the clichés and shared understandings of what a home is?

The fourth chapter, "Sharing a Meal," begins with the common experience of having meals together with family or friends. It looks more closely at the power relations and gender roles that often give daily meals a ritual nature. How do two people from different family backgrounds negotiate shared dining customs? How does a family reconcile cultural, class, and personal differences during special meals like Christmas and Thanksgiving? The chapter discusses how one can explore the thin boundary between the real and the ideal. One way is to observe the subtle ways that conflicts are concealed and channeled, creating "zones of avoidance" and "taboo topics" as dangers that must be navigated. Another way is to study cases of miscommunications, founded on a false assumption of shared culture.

Chapter 5 is called "Do You Remember Facebook?" and deals with the uses of domestic media, illustrating how objects, technologies, and skills become invisible as a given part of daily life. The focus here is on people learning and unlearning ways to handle all kinds of electronic gadgets. The contemporary uses of or enthusiasm about new media is problematized by comparing with older generations and practices. The chapter opens with a visit to the basement burial ground of old media stuff, from family albums to music cassettes. One theme is how you can study people's life histories through interactions with domestic media.

The sixth chapter, "Catching a Mood," uses an ethnography of a railway station and commuter life to illustrate how a dialogue between reading literature and doing fieldwork evolves. It shows how any ethnographic exploration is shaped and framed by the understanding that is brought into the field. "Start in the library" is vague advice often given to students, but by reading all kinds of materials (from academic studies to fiction or advertisements), as well as surfing the Net (from blogs to YouTube), the ethnography will be more interesting. By mixing observations and interviews with a constant search for other materials, it is possible to return to the field with new ideas. This chapter also illustrates how the six senses can all be put into an ethnography to capture the elusive nature of a passing mood or a particular local atmosphere.

"Crafting Wood and Words" is the title of the seventh chapter, which takes documenting a do-it-yourself project of carpentry as a starting point to understand how writing and ethnography are intertwined. Writing is not something that follows *after* collecting material and analyzing it. The making of a study is actually about the constant interweaving of writing, ethnography, and analysis from day one. Documenting and analyzing an episode of home carpentry is demonstrated through the parallel process of crafting words and experimenting with different styles of writing.

The eighth chapter, "Demystifying Fieldwork," looks at how research is organized in daily activities. While older electronic tools are collecting dust in the basement, new devices for recording and communicating information are changing the practices of ethnography. Comparing changes in cultural research over the last decades, it is possible to see how methods were shaped by old and new media and by different academic norms and habits.

The final chapter, "Taking Cultural Analysis Out into the World," deals with life after university. Today's students must often find new arenas of employment. There is a rising interest in applied cultural analysis of the everyday in many sectors including corporations, government institutions, and NGOs. How can the skills of cultural analysis and ethnography be put to work in different job settings? What tools does a researcher bring there and what are the most efficient and expressive ways to present the results of cultural analysis to various audiences?

Unlike practitioners of medicine or law, students trained in cultural analysis often find it hard to present and formulate their special skills to a prospective employer or an interdisciplinary research team. We show how this can be done, drawing on interviews with students who have made the transformation into the working world in diverse circumstances. We also discuss what skills employers look for—above all, the knack of being able to say something surprising about the far-too-well-known aspects of life, using interesting materials and innovative angles.

2

THE IMPORTANCE OF SMALL THINGS

My boyfriend and I have been talking for five months about moving in together. Both of us feel that we have a wonderful relationship and that we are very happy together. Right now we each live in separate one-room apartments, so we don't have the opportunity to test out cohabitation in advance. We simply have to get our own apartment.

Now I wonder if it's usual to move in together when you have only been a couple for so short a time. Actually it's long enough, in that we already know each other rather well and have learnt about each other's strengths and shortcomings. But I have never felt like this about a man so early before.

I also wonder, HOW do you actually do it? Okay, you move your stuff and live at the same address, but HOW? There must be special problems that every couple has when they move in together, but what are they? How do you avoid them? Do you have any tips about how to make this go as smoothly and as easily as possible? Surely discussions must come up about the toothbrush, the wardrobe, and who will be master in the house?

We found quotes like this one on the home page of a website on getting married. What is really going on when couples in love move in together? How do cultural researchers tackle this question that not only occupies many people in their everyday lives but is also a popular subject in all kinds of media—from web blogs to soap operas?

In this chapter we will sketch out an investigation of the first time that a couple moves in together. The focus is on ways of quickly starting a study and then moving on toward the finished product.

Doing ethnography and cultural analysis is usually a messy business. It is only in the final written version that it may appear as a well-organized task. Here, however, we will describe this untidy research process as if it consisted of five clearly defined steps: starting out, searching for literature, collecting empirical data, analysis, and writing. In actual research these "steps" are usually undertaken in any order. The fifth step, writing, is where you actually begin—in the form of improvised notes and ideas. Likewise, the first step, the start, is something that is repeated several times. When you get stuck, you have to find ways of restarting your study. Analysis does not happen only after the collection of the material; like the writing, it goes on all the time.

THE FIRST STEP: GETTING GOING

In the world of handbooks, you begin an investigation by deciding on your aim and your research questions. There are often clear instructions for the writing of an academic paper or a report: you should set out by explaining what you are going to explore and the methods and theories that will be used. Other research on the subject will be presented. Order, clarity, and logic are the cornerstones in such instructions.

But, as we mentioned, actual research is seldom so systematic. The work process, from the first ideas to the final text, is, in fact, rather unpredictable. The more you get to know about your topic, the more complicated it becomes. Now and again, both the purpose and the direction of the investigation are changed by unexpected information. You have to constantly make choices about which direction to go, and some roads turn out to be dead ends. Doing cultural research is therefore an adventure, a mixture of academic traditions and routines, insecurity, and surprises.

At the start, you have to get a general view of the field and ask productive questions. Are couples moving in together heterosexual or homosexual, young or old, rich or poor? What are their ethnic, cultural, and social backgrounds? Where are they moving, to a new shared place or where one of them already lives? Are they moving directly from the parental home or from some other relationship? Many similar questions function as fuel for your research and turn you into an ethnographer that looks for all kinds of information everywhere. This is where the bricolage approach comes in.

In our own case, we began by Googling "moving in together." We ended up in an Internet forum where people discussed themes as in the quote we began with. Most of the answers to these questions about moving in together were not as specific as we had expected. Rather, they gave couples more general advice: do not quarrel before you go to bed, be in agreement on the economy, and be honest with each other. For sure, this is important wisdom for a working cohabitation, but it is also too predictable. On the Internet, and in conversations with people, there is a tendency to reproduce standard wisdoms and old clichés—rather like an echo chamber. There are so many "shoulds" and "musts."

Instead we looked for smaller things, "the trifles" as someone on the forum called them. "He TOUCHES THE CHEESE! with his fingers! Unbelievable!" Such petty details open up new perspectives, as when somebody

Figure 2.1. Ethnographic observation means looking hard at even the most inconspicuous detail. It can suddenly reveal a surprise. (Adina Ehn)

writes that "he doesn't like it when I don't hang up the pot-holders after having used them, while I don't like it when he puts the butter in the icebox together with the knife"; or, "the worst thing he knows is hair in the washbasin."

Where should you put the pot of honey? Can you mix cheese and jam on the bread? Is it okay to save all the newspapers and read them a week later, or to surf the web all night? What is the proper way of tying a plastic bag, and how do you survive when your partner doesn't clean the toilet? Trifles, yes, but it is such small, more-or-less-neglected matters that everyday life is full of and that may wear out the most passionate relationship.

On another online discussion forum on "family life," we looked at answers to the question, what are "things that your boy/girlfriend does that make you annoyed?" Besides that "he has a flagpole in his arse and never turns the light off in the bathroom," there were almost five hundred other examples of different reasons to get irritated with your partner. Certainly rich material for research that also makes us wonder how people manage to live together at all. But this is not the main question in our planned investigation. Nor will we explore such topics as romantic love, sexuality, or the desire for children. Right now we are more interested in what different couples do, and how, with all their stuff, habits, and routines when they are going to share a home. Our research focus is on the importance of minor, mostly inconspicuous, matters. By looking at these, we want to learn more about where and how the boundaries in a new relationship are drawn between "mine," "yours," and "ours." Who takes or gets the power over what?

Such questions are connected with one of our most essential ethnographic and analytical tools: the concentration on *actions* and *events*. Instead of asking directly what people think or feel, we look for what they *do* or have done. Their concrete experiences are more exciting for us than are their opinions and attitudes, which often may be rather predictable. One vital aim of cultural research is to be surprised.

THE SECOND STEP: SEARCHING FOR LITERATURE

Now it's time to visit the Internet, bookstores, and libraries, and to browse through lists of references in books and articles, but also to ask other people for tips. This kind of search may take you to unexpected authors and ideas. One clue leads to another, and it is important to remember that different kinds of search engines give different results. Try Googling and then letting your finger run along the spines of library collections. When you play on the Net with various word combinations—such as "move together/ethnography/habits/cleaning"—you may get surprising material that directs your investigation into unknown terrains, just as opening a book taken at random from a bookstore shelf may yield unforeseen information.

We began with some earlier research. In a study of young Danish couples, the ethnologist Sarah Holst Kjær (2009) follows them from the kitchen sink and the bathroom to the TV sofa. She shows how important it is for the couples to synchronize their individual habits into common routines and to find a shared rhythm. There are lots of discussions about what kinds of everyday behavior they find "immensely irritating." At the same time, male and female stereotypes are reproduced and often used as arguments for what is essential or not. Who takes the role of the expert on how things should be done in the kitchen and what kinds of arguments about right or wrong are used? In this early maneuvering, long-standing divisions of labor or hierarchies of routines may be established.

As households develop steady patterns of practices, there are still divergences; even the smallest ones can drive you crazy. There was the couple that waged a constant battle about the door to the kitchen. As surely as the husband kept it open, the wife would close it with an irritated slam. Their different routines turned out to have to do with their class backgrounds. He had grown up in a working-class family where the kitchen was the center of the home, where everybody congregated and all kinds of activities occurred. Whereas in her upper-class childhood, the kitchen was a territory strictly reserved for cooking and the smell of food seeping through into the rest of the apartment was a sign of vulgarity.

Sarah Holst Kjær also explored negotiations about whose rules and routines should be applied. Trifling matters such as the order in the kitchen drawers, or the amount of computer gaming, may suddenly become causes for conflict that make the relationship insecure or produce feelings of uneasiness. When the day is over, the two lovers may lie silently in bed, their eyes wide open, as in a Hollywood movie, while one anxiously asks: "What are you thinking about?"

Another book that we found helpful was written by the French sociologist Jean-Claude Kaufmann (2002). It is an interview study about "the first morning," where people recollect the start of a new relationship. They remember how it felt to wake up in a new setting in what may be the first morning of a lifelong relationship or just a temporary love affair. As two strangers beginning to share their everyday life together, they often find themselves wandering into a minefield where the tiniest routine may become endearing or provocative. For some of the interviewed couples the magic of romance makes anything acceptable, while others keep an eye on the new partner's morning routines in order to find out if this is the kind of person they are ready to live with. Colombine remembers that first morning:

> *In the beginning this was an unknown house, with strange drawers and food you normally wouldn't eat—it was a journey of discovery, a total discovery.*

She carefully enters the bathroom, checks the fridge, and secretly glances at the photos on the drawer. As a guest in this new morning universe, she is cautious and lets her new partner choose the breakfast menu and give the morning its shape and rhythm.

Anna wakes up surrounded by her new partner's family. In spite of the friendly atmosphere she is trying to make herself as invisible as possible, all the time afraid she will embarrass herself. Every gadget or task seems a potential trap. For Vincent, it was not until the third day that he realized he had committed a deadly sin by using the left-hand washbasin in the bathroom. It was strictly reserved for the father of the house and the rest of the family had to use the other one on the right. "I thought this was comical, I just couldn't get it," he remembers.

The new couple watches each other's behavior, and adapts, or gets annoyed. Many feel petty in their judgments of the other person's habits; even the smallest detail gathers great importance. Is it right to shower after breakfast? Can one blow one's nose on a piece of toilet paper? What is seen as cute, and what seems awkward or, perhaps, even revolting?

As morning follows morning, routines are established or changed. What kinds of habits are you ready to compromise on? As the first intense passion fades away, the tolerance for what is seen as strange behavior diminishes. You no longer want to live as a guest.

When Isa visited Tristan she felt like a different Isa who accepted the strangest habits, such as having spaghetti and cheese for breakfast or the very slow rhythm of his morning routines. But the day she decided to move in with him, she began to see his habits with new eyes: "As I opened my suitcase, I felt like changing everything according to my own needs." Others tell how it was through confrontations like these that they realized how obsessed they were with their own routines. Why were they so immensely important?

As new couples build up a daily life together, accommodating their respective interests and habits, they create a shared choreography of working together in the kitchen and having a certain order in the bathroom. In this process, another aspect of routines comes into the foreground: their potential as a battlefield. Since they most often are taken for granted and anchored in the body, it is no little thing if they are challenged, as happens in new domestic partnerships. "They are just a part of me!"

We also look for examples and ideas in novels, autobiographies, and self-help literature. Even when you open a book just for the enjoyment of reading you may find usable material, as when one of us read the musician Patti Smith's *Just Kids* (2009). In this autobiographical memoir, she writes about the tough early years of her career and her life with the photographic artist Robert Mapplethorpe in a tiny flat in Manhattan. Initially, there was no intention to use her story for research purposes. It was only afterward that it became apparent that she does in fact relate many interesting things about the pleasures and troubles of moving in together.

In spite of the fact that Patti and Robert were broke and constantly starving, they had each other and they had their art. With very scarce means, they built a home together that they both liked. They cleaned, washed, painted, and spread out their few belongings in the narrow space. In the beginning, they slept on the floor with winter coats as a mattress.

> *I went back to South Jersey and retrieved my books and clothing. While I was gone Robert hung his drawings and draped the walls with Indian cloth. He dressed the mantel with religious artifacts, candles, and souvenirs from the Day of the Dead, arranging as if sacred objects on an altar. Finally he prepared a study area for me with a little worktable and the frayed magic carpet.*
>
> *We combined our belongings. My few records were filed in the orange crate with his. My winter coat hung next to his sheepskin vest.* (Smith 2009: 44)

With the help of such descriptions we looked for comparative material. By searching in both academic research and fiction, we found more varied examples. Of course you have to reflect on the differences between these two forms of producing knowledge. A novel might open your eyes to new aspects of your research problem and inspire productive questions, but it cannot be used in the same way as examples from empirical research. You have to make it clear in which way you are using the literary examples: as vivid illustrations, as kind of preliminary assumptions, or as starting points for further ethnographic explorations.

When planning our small study of couples moving in together, we find ourselves experiencing a special sensitivity for the subject. Suddenly, much in our surroundings seems to be dealing with the same thing—in movies, newspapers and magazines, TV programs, songs, and in common chat. We collect experiences of sharing a place with somebody from students, friends, and acquaintances. This means that ethnography and cultural analysis are more or less constantly ongoing activities.

When searching for examples in media and literature, how do you know what is usable? In our case, as we have said, we look for everyday activities and concrete small matters, those things that often are disregarded as less important but which may, in fact, drive people crazy and cause major quarrels—or, as in the case of Patti Smith and Robert Mapplethorpe, unite the couple.

THE THIRD STEP: COLLECTING MATERIAL

In many handbooks you can learn how to collect or produce empirical material through traditional fieldwork methods such as interviewing, observing, photographing, or making questionnaires. Doing "netnography" and reading fiction are other possibilities. Fieldwork can also be "translocal" or "multi-sited," where you follow actors, objects, or a given phenomenon. You may, for example, study homemaking by following concepts of "the ideal home" or "the perfect couple" as they travel between different settings, from self-help books and interior decoration magazines to soap operas. Or you could follow such ideas through history. How did the images of the perfect home look back in the early 2000s, the 1950s, or a century ago? You may follow commuters between the scenes of home and work, the migrants who have double homes; or you may decide to follow the "micro-moves" of domestic stuff, traveling between the basement and the living room, for example.

A good strategy is to begin with simple things, as the sociologist Christina Nippert-Eng does in her book *Islands of Privacy* (2010). She sets out to investigate how the borderlines are drawn between privacy and public life in society. Everybody has opinions about this, but if all you do is ask them about it, you probably receive rather stereotypical answers that mirror the media debate, which does not tell us much about how this dilemma is actually managed in everyday life.

Therefore, Nippert-Eng begins with the purse and the wallet. She simply asks people to empty their purses or wallets and to organize the contents into two heaps—one for strictly private matters, and one for other things. Then she asks them to physically handle the objects and to tell her about what led them to place each item in one or the other of the categories. By utilizing everyday things in this way, Nippert-Eng found it to be a good and relaxed way of opening an interview about more difficult topics. We will present some other similar research techniques, which may also be effective in kick-starting an investigation: autoethnography, improvised short interviews, and spontaneous questionnaires.

Autoethnography, nowadays an established method, means using your own experiences as research material. What happened the first time my partner and I created a home together? Which belongings did I bring; how did I behave when we chose the furniture; how did we adjust our habits? Who decided about curtains, bookshelves, and kitchen fixtures? Were there any trifling issues that turned into touchy ones? Searching for such memories, reactions, and feelings will make it possible to design questions to ask others.

Long and penetrating interviews are, of course, a well-tested method in social and cultural research. But in the preliminary stage of an investigation, you may also use more *informal conversations* as a way of getting information. You can ask your friends, parents, or relatives about what happened when they started living with somebody. What about the china, the icebox, the books, the records, the plants, the paintings? Did you discuss how to share the cleaning and the cooking? Should one sleep with the bedroom window open or closed?

In this way you collect several stories about moving in together; for example, about the first day, the first bed, the first Christmas—or the first quarrel. Such quick "interviews" can be carried out wherever and whenever, during a coffee break, at a party, or taking a walk. Helping others to move, by carrying furniture, you may combine questioning with observations. How is the couple agreeing on the arranging of their new home? The purpose is, again, to get very concrete information about the importance of small things.

A third technique to begin an investigation is to make *spontaneous questionnaires*, for example, on Facebook. In our case, we used another quick method. We asked students to write down answers to a given question on a slip of paper. What about your experiences of waiting or daydreaming? What do you find very odd in daily life? How old do you feel? What are your experiences of moving in with somebody? The students wrote down their answers anonymously and provided us with a lot of examples of culturally influenced behavior. Many of the answers about moving in with someone concerned order and cleaning:

> *All these dirty socks everywhere—is this the way it should be?*
> *I was cleaning all the time, and she thought that this was very remarkable.*
> *My wife lets her clothes lie on the floor.*
> *My boyfriend does not throw empty toilet paper rolls in the garbage.*

He gets annoyed when I just crumple up the supermarket plastic bags in a drawer without folding them.
The first few times it felt odd to vacuum in front of my boyfriend.

Others wrote about how to hang the dishcloth, where to put the tube of toothpaste, and the place for the remote controls. Someone was irritated by their partner spreading themselves out on the TV sofa, or, again, when he lays the butter knife down in the butter packet and puts it all away into the icebox.

Another area of disputes was cooking: liking or disliking different dishes, for example. If one loves garlic and the other hates it, it will be difficult to agree in the kitchen. Several answers were rather emotional, such as this one:

Something that is fucking annoying is that he can never eat ordinary food. It must always be so awfully special and complicated, gratinated blah blah blah with broccoli. Why not just have some sausage and macaroni when both of us are tired and bored?

Time and planning is a usual stumbling block when you live together, especially when you have different diurnal rhythms: when one of you is alert in the morning and tired toward the evening, while the other is the very opposite. One person in the couple wishes to plan everything in good time, while the other takes each day as it comes. It can be "madly irritating" when one partner is always putting off the cleaning and postponing everything, or only cooks when she or he gets hungry.

People that move in together early in their relationship may discover that the partner has interests they had not noticed before. While one plays computer games every evening, the other wants to be together and talk. One of the students complained that her boyfriend brought his pals around whenever he wanted without any prior warning. "His hobby turned out to be his whole life," someone else wrote laconically, without revealing what the hobby was exactly.

With the help of autoethnographic insights, short interviews, and spontaneous questionnaires, we get some very varied information to work with. It is probably not enough for writing an essay, but it is a good start. Of course, we need to reflect about what kinds of situations and experiences they represent. What kinds of worlds do the fifty answers given by young college students or a few improvised interviews with relatives stand for?

Now it is time to make a choice about how to continue. Quick interviews can be developed into longer and more-systematic ones, and again there are many ways of interviewing to choose between. We find "the walk-along" useful: following a couple around their new home, handling stuff, and trying out sofas while talking. One could also decide to turn the study into an analysis

Figure 2.2. Everywhere people try to create order, organizing stuff into categories, drawing boundaries they take for granted. (Richard Wilk)

of norms and ideals for homemaking, which means looking at media such as self-help books, advertisements, and furniture catalogues.

But how much material do you need and how can a bricolage method of combining different sources create a good enough platform for doing the study? There is also the classic question of how many interviews you are supposed to do. When is the media material you have gathered sufficient? The answers to these questions are not simple. It depends, of course, on what kind of investigation you are making, whether it is for a smaller exercise, a longer paper, or a thesis.

In qualitative research, there is a rule of thumb that fewer and more deep-probing interviews are better than a greater number of short ones. The important thing is not only the amount of information but also how it is examined and what kind of knowledge you want to produce. For example, in a cultural analysis of couples moving in together, the purpose usually is not to decide what is normal but to show through concrete examples how people with different circumstances are managing the situation. How do different cultural backgrounds, for example, produce different behavior? Again, it is what people are actually *doing* that catches our interest, and that is not always the same as what they *say* that they are doing.

THE FOURTH STEP: THE ANALYSIS

Analysis calls for hard thinking to look at a phenomenon from different directions, to use theoretical concepts, and to be prepared to draw conclusions other than those you had expected. For example, if you analyze moving in together from a gender perspective, you ask what significance ideas about male and female behavior have when creating a new home. Which roles and expectations influence the interaction? What kind of power order is established? Addressing issues such as class and ethnicity calls for questions about the social, cultural, and economic backgrounds of the couple. What kind of cultural baggage did they bring with them from their respective families of origin? How do they think, feel, and act concerning money? Do religious beliefs and rituals have any importance?

Cultural analysis means turning over very concrete matters again and again, trying to catch the well-known in a new light. You get very close to your subject, and in the next moment, you look at it from a distance. You ask new questions about the petty details. What do dirty socks mean in a love relationship? Why is it so important where the butter knife is put?

To ask productive questions you need analytical tools that help to link small matters with large issues. Let us shortly outline some of these tools, some of which we will return to in other chapters.

In order to make everyday activities such as routines visible, it is helpful to search for analytical conflicts or pivotal moments as well as for contrasting examples. Looking for *break points* is about finding moments in everyday life when things taken for granted are suddenly questioned. This is an analytical method to tease out new and often unexpected dimensions in mundane activities. You may, as Jean-Claude Kaufmann did in his study of couples moving in together, concentrate on situations when inconspicuous routines bump into each other—my good habits, for example, against your strange behavior.

The second theme, using *contrasts*, is about finding ways to distance yourself from the phenomenon you are studying by using cultural settings in other places or times. A historical perspective may give such a critical distance. What is a home? Or how do you define an intimate relationship in other kinds of cultural contexts? Sometimes just a generational comparison is enough to show how easy it is to take something as given. What was it like to move in to live together in the 1960s? Are working-class and middle-class ideas of homemaking similar?

Another analytical tool is to focus on culture as *learning processes*. This means looking at everyday practices and ideas as something people learn to share, making what may be experienced as something very personal or individual a more general cultural pattern. By exploring how people acquire habits, ideas, and skills, it is possible to understand how everyday life is made and remade all the time and how basic social values or norms are hidden in seemingly trivial practices. A good example is the anthropologist Adrie Kusserow's (2004) ethnographic studies of how American preschool children learn about class and come to reproduce class positions. In her ethnography of different day-care centers, she shows how class is learned in unobtrusive and often unconscious ways. Bodily hints, tacit messages, and all kinds of small cultural cues are incorporated as a set of dispositions and orientations—a physical habitus, a concept Kusserow borrows from the sociologist Pierre Bourdieu.

A focus on inconspicuous ways of learning to handle the everyday means interviewing young couples about how they navigate their way together during the early stages of their homemaking. Before you have gotten used to each other, everyday life together becomes an adventure where you try to create common routines and rhythms, and to negotiate about alternatives concerning practical matters.

A fourth theme concerns the importance of *emotions*. Why is it that some simple routines can provoke strong feelings? When there is a strong emotional charge in a seemingly trivial situation, it is a signal that something important is going on: a shrug, an ironic aside, a bored expression, or a passionate interest. Focusing on the emotional dimensions of everyday life is a way of discovering cultural investments about good or bad habits, or right or wrong ways of doing things.

In love relationships, emotions are, of course, crucial. They can emerge at any time as powerful forces—anger, joy, or a longing for something else. They announce that something important is going on, as when the couple in Sarah Holst Kjær's earlier-mentioned investigation explodes in a quarrel about the kitchen door: will it be shut or not? This leads us to wonder what emotional expressions stand for and what purpose they have in a relationship. What is the lovers' discussion about cleaning matters really about?

Finally, it is often rewarding to explore the *materialities* of everyday life. On the domestic scene, both ordinary objects and physical surroundings are important coactors in social life. In their constant everyday doings, people interact with material objects in many different ways—as memory carriers, scarce resources, or makers of atmospheres. What, for example, can we learn from observing how people handle material stuff when they are furnishing their home, or sharing the space and taking care of their belongings? How does the battle over the remote controls develop? How are souvenirs and cherished belongings charged with emotions that unite or divide the couple? Such questions again force us to notice the importance of tiny matters in everyday life. Both the dimensions of emotionality and materiality also direct the attention to activities and reactions that often are hard to verbalize, even if you are aware of them.

To conclude, these five themes turned out to be helpful in developing a study of what may happen when couples move in together. By not primarily looking for general ideas about ideals or conventions of couple-making but, instead, looking for inconspicuous details—the dirty socks appearing in wrong places or plastic bags folded incorrectly—it is possible to find new analytical entrances to a field that many people think they already know all too well.

This attention to small things may produce new perspectives on large issues. How are gender hierarchies reproduced or challenged in everyday routines? How are intimacy and distance given cultural forms? In the heated statements we encountered in discussions on the Internet or in interviews, routines about food, cleaning, and order in the home kept appearing often. Moving in together is not only about organizing a new everyday life. It is also about understandings of selfhood, boundaries of the body, and other sensitive issues. In the beginning of a relationship, a loving couple may share both toothbrush and towel—for a while. Battles about the order in the kitchen drawers, clothes on the floor, and eating preferences give insights into basic cultural ideas and ideals. They also show how conflicts may mirror social differences or how gender conceptions are confirmed or questioned, in everything from cleaning to who takes care of the contacts with relatives.

As cultural analysts, our aim is not to understand the psychology of couple-making but to see it in terms of culture: learned and shared practices, or ideas that are typical of a certain setting, as with the middle-class youngsters of Copenhagen in Sarah Holst Kjær's study.

THE FIFTH STEP: WRITING

The last of the steps may just as well be called the first. Writing starts from day one with hunches, wild ideas, questions that could be developed—all should go into the notebook or the computer file. At this stage, ignorance can be used as a resource. It is permitted to be naïve and to ask silly questions—nobody else will read it. Later on, some of the scribbles may be shown to contain productive thoughts. Writing is thus a part of both collecting/producing material and of analyzing it. Ideas may circulate in the head, but they need to be put down into written text. To many cultural researchers, writing actually *is* the investigation. It is by searching for words, building sentences, deleting, and rewriting that you think and move ahead.

Our advice to students is simple: just begin to write! Don't wait for brilliant ideas and surprising knowledge. Write to get something to think with. It's like climbing the stairs; you do it step-by-step. What you write today will work as a new step for tomorrow's writing. All of a sudden you will have the peculiar but liberating experience of writing something that will surprise you. Writing is a creative process that you don't have total control over; it is guided by emotions and fantasies in unexpected ways—at the same time as you are expected to follow methodological rules. There is a constant balancing act between more detached and impersonal writing and the creative search for new ideas. The final text is a combination of both.

❖

In the five steps that we have described, different tools are mixed in a methodological bricolage. Some of them are suitable as tools for starting out; others are used at a later stage for developing the analysis or for a critical control of the early conclusions. The fragmentary answers from the spontaneous questionnaire raise new questions that you may ask in longer interviews in order to get a clearer and broader perspective. Autoethnography and reading novels inspire you to look for concrete examples in unexpected places and situations.

In the following chapters we will develop this methodological strategy by discussing some very different kinds of studies. New research utensils will be added to the toolbox, but they are used for the same basic purpose. By beginning with small things and mundane matters, the aim is to be led into larger issues. What may seem as a detour or an unused side entrance can add new and surprising dimensions to everyday practices we think we already know inside and out.

3

MAKING THE FAMILIAR STRANGE

Cultural researchers are supposed to be able to look at familiar phenomena with "new eyes," turning the mundane into the exotic. A good case of something so well-known that it is a real challenge to see it in a new light is the home—for example, the place of living that the couples in the previous chapter were making.

This time we will use the home to develop analytical strategies for questioning what is taken for granted, and we will discuss how we have tried different entrances to this topic. Is it possible to look at one's own home in order to discover something new and strange there? And what about in other people's homes? It is hard to suppress one's curiosity when invited into a new home; we check out the furnishings or the pictures on the wall, comparing tastes, but it is a long step from there to thinking about a home as a cultural construction, a set of symbols, or a way of living.

To make oneself a stranger to the familiar and become surprised by the ordinary is a demanding task that calls for practice as well as unconventional methods and analytical tools. You have to be prepared with well-thought-out questions as well as letting yourself be open to the unexpected. How is it possible to expand the capacity to look with fresh eyes at everyday life, wherever it is performed? Our particular case is the home, but the strategies we use could be set to work to understand many other overly familiar elements. It could be a study of a workplace, a daily commute, or a shopping trip (see Ehn and Löfgren 2010 for more examples).

MAKING A FIRST ATTEMPT

The first step is to define the subject of study, which might be more difficult than it seems. "Home" turns out to be a very elusive concept with many different shapes and meanings. Open the door to any home, and what will you be stumbling over as you enter? Furniture and personal belongings, of course, but you will also get entangled in all the domestic routines and emotions hiding inside.

"What defines a home?" the anthropologist Mary Douglas (1991) once asked. She points out that it is not just a building with four walls, but something of an internal order with rules, habits, and rhythms. The home is above all a web of routines, of silent agreements, and ingrained reflexes about "the ways we do things here." Here people have learned how to survive a stressful morning, how to store the food in the fridge or quarrel over the laundry, and much, much more. An important point is that at first sight the home seems so intensely material. It is full of stuff, but so much of what organizes this stuff and makes it into a home is invisible: the flow of routines and emotions, the dreams and ideals that are hiding in the sofa or are stuffed away in the drawer.

The bricolage method is a good way to look for a broad mixture of materials and perspectives. Material on domestic living turns up everywhere: in total-makeover TV shows; in blogs and in newspaper debates on what is called "the current craze for interior decoration." Homemaking is demonstrated in furniture catalogues and magazines. It is analyzed in art projects as well as in research from a wide range of disciplines.

Let us begin by collecting all kinds of "home" words and reflect over their changing meanings: homelike, homemade, home bird, home-felt, homespun, homesickness, and home truths. While walking the streets, we gaze inquisitively into apartments that are dark or lit up and we fantasize about what goes on in there. How should we interpret broken Venetian blinds, drooping pot plants, or perfectly designed curtain arrangements? What do the visible and material things say about the home or about our prejudices? As home birds with different social backgrounds, we have been filled by ideas and norms about what a good or interesting home should look like. Like few other concepts, the home carries strong ideological charges.

It doesn't take long to realize that we have embarked on a gigantic project. It has been treated so often in media, movies, novels, and even research that it seems to be almost impossible to say something surprising and exciting about it. We also discover that the concepts "home" and "at home" are not at all clear and self-evident. Now is the time to ask some very basic and naïve questions—such as when, where, and how is "a home," and for whom? Such questions make us see the differences between a house, an apartment, a household, a family, and a home—concepts that often are mixed up as synonyms. It is important to separate physical structures, practical activities, and social relations on the one hand, and dreams, ideals, memories, and emotions on the other.

Just think about what you are actually seeing when you read and look at the pictures in home furnishing magazines. In the text, people talk about and

Figure 3.1.   **Suddenly you see something that captures your curiosity. What is going on in front of this church in Venice? What does it mean? You may start guessing or boldly ask the guys what they are up to. Who knows what story you will hear? (Billy Ehn)**

show their "homes," but what we actually see is walls, floors, ceilings, furniture, decorations, and other material objects. We also read about dreams, home improvements, and the search for special things. But where is *the home* in all this? We have to conclude that a place in which to live is not necessarily the same as a home and that it is possible to feel at home practically anywhere. A house or an apartment may produce many different experiences and meanings for the people living there, and you can never be sure in advance what those experiences and meanings are. For the cultural researcher, the home has to be discovered—every time.

The idea is to explore the way people themselves experience and understand their environment, the dynamic ways in which everyday life creates a home and makes it meaningful to those who inhabit it. This makes the home stand out as the result of repeated practices as well as a sensory totality.

LOOKING FOR ENTRANCES

What about other studies that may provide inspiration and ideas about how to explore our topic? From the vast literature on "home," we begin with three books that use ethnographic methods to do creative research. They are about the practical, material, and emotional aspects of life in different homes, and they touch on some of the analytical themes we have mentioned earlier. Their focus is on what people are *doing* and *feeling* at home.

Our first example teaches us how to study the home through actions and feelings. In *Home Possessions*, Daniel Miller (2001) and his coresearchers describe and analyze homes in different countries more as social and cultural processes than as physical places. With the help of interviews, narratives, observations, maps, pictures, and drawings, they try to understand what a home means to different people, both now and in the past, and what people do at home with their furniture and other possessions. They are also interested in what people take with them when they move and how they sort things out.

One of the chapters is especially useful. Pauline Garvey (2001) looks at how people move furniture around and how feelings can be changed by shifting the sofa or cleaning the kitchen. She is interested in finding out why people—some more than others—are constantly moving stuff around and redecorating. What does all this shifting and rearranging do to the emotional tone of the home and to the people dragging the things around, critically trying to reinvent their home? Seemingly banal routines such as buying a new candlestick or changing the cushions on the sofa might be experienced as giving the home a new "feel."

Simply observing people rearranging their apartment, or asking what effect doing this has on them, may open up several questions. On the one hand, it can be about feelings of never being content, about being aware of the outside pressures to constantly upgrade and improve the home. Such a perspective calls for an analysis of how people are influenced by fashions and changing ideals as well as by marketing campaigns. On the other hand, the focus can move to how routines of rearranging and cleaning out have more to do with the need to be active. Can the ritual of reshuffling domestic objects also be seen as a reorganizing of one's own life? Such an analysis needs to engage with questions of gender, generation, and class. Are women, as Garvey shows, more into this constant rearranging than men, and if so, why? A detailed ethnographic study of thirty-two Californian homes, overflowing with objects and activities, can give further inspiration for studying this (see Arnold et al. 2012). In the first home the researchers visited, they found over two thousand visible objects in three rooms. Later, when doing interviews, they realized that it was mainly the wives who kept worrying about the threatening excess of domestic stuff.

The second example is about the sensual home as a research object. In Sarah Pink's *Home Truths* (2004), it is the sensory dimension of home that is emphasized. She uses interviews, observations, and video films to capture those sights, sounds, smells, and tastes that characterize home in England and Spain. The result is a visual and sensory ethnography of housework, from a comparative perspective. Pink stands in kitchens and watches people wash the dishes; she talks with them about their views on order and cleanliness, and she analyzes their body language in her videos.

Here, again, home is not just a living place but also an agency, something that is done, practiced, alone or together with other people. It is described as a material, sensual, emotional, and imagined identity-space. For Pink, the comparative perspective works well and helps her to see how homes can be produced in very different settings. She walks on different flooring and smells different foods cooking as well as the lingering odors of cleaning products or of old chests of drawers. She is constantly checking how all the senses take in information about different homes. It is very much about registering atmospheres (a theme we will return to in a later chapter) and describing how light, humidity, temperature, sounds, and smells work together.

One central question for Pink is how gender is produced along with the material and sensory environments. She found that both men and women perform different sorts of masculinities and femininities in their domestic creativity—for example, in small rituals like dancing while vacuuming or juggling the dishes while washing them.

Pink stresses especially the female experiences of authority as homemakers. They are said to express themselves by decorating their homes and trying to create an atmosphere. Some of them say that they see their homes as "sanctuaries," where they can do as they like and wear what they want. This opens up the interesting tension of the home as both a showcase *to* the world and a private shelter *from* the world.

Pink's approach tells us about the importance of contrasts in cultural analysis. By going to Spain she gains new insights into aspects of domestic living in England. It evokes a classic analytical approach—such as when you compare similar apartments in a high-rise building furnished and used by people of very different backgrounds. You walk through the same living rooms, but the choices of furniture and the rooms' functions differ. The family with a Middle East background on the third floor has arranged all the sofas along the walls and doesn't use the Western tradition of a dining room table, thereby creating a very different landscape for socializing. The retired couple from the American Midwest has created a rural, almost timeless, atmosphere in their apartment on the eighth floor. The single mother on the thirteenth floor has neither the time nor the money to keep redecorating; here, it is the needs of the children and their activities that shape the home.

A simple way of trying this contrastive method is to look at two homes that represent different generations or lifestyles, or to think of a typical non-home as a contrast: a hotel room or a temporary refugee camp, perhaps.

A third approach is using people's own ways of describing or picturing their homes. Here, our example is the Danish anthropologist Ida Wentzel Winther's (2006) study of "homeliness," or the ways in which people make themselves at home, or not, in domestic spaces. Her aim is to find out how people, especially children, describe and experience their homes. She gives twenty-four eleven-year-old boys and girls disposable cameras to take pictures in their homes. Then she walks through the rooms with the children asking them questions about the pictures they chose to take and what they mean. She recognizes their choices of motives from home magazines and furniture catalogues. The children seem to be familiar with the IKEA way of presenting home as a living place. Again, this opens up the question of how we learn to see a home not only by living in it but also by taking into account the constant barrage of ideals, fashions, and trends in homemaking coming from the outside world.

The children's photographs are mostly devoid of people; the possessions stand for the home. But when they talk about their pictures, they fill them with details of everyday life, and they tell about what they actually do in the different rooms. Long dialogues are quoted where the children explain the meaning of chairs, beds, house pets, the fridge, beautiful things, tables, couches, doors, windows, and many other things. They talk about smells and sounds, and about all the rules at home. What is forbidden and what is allowed? Can you eat in front of the TV? Is it okay to answer your cell phone while eating? Are you allowed to play in the kitchen or not? Who makes the decisions about each matter?

The children also reflect on how they make themselves feel at home. Withdrawing to their room with a book and a bag of sweets, they create their own universe with the help of a warming blanket and some favorite music. "This is when I feel most at home!"

Wentzel Winther's approach could be developed in several directions. What if one asked different members of the household to describe their shared home? Would this produce different versions, different kinds of focus and sentiments? How is a home viewed through the lenses of not only gender but also age?

Another striking element in the children's photographs is the focus on special items of furniture, such as the dining table and the TV couch. This inspires us to ask very elementary questions. What is a table? What can it be used for? A table is not only a piece of woodwork; it is also a cultural object with strong symbolic and emotional charges. It is in some ways a very demanding object, with rules and routines for use that vary between different cultural settings. Just by photographing or videotaping a kitchen table around the clock, it is possible to see how many activities and objects fight for space there.

A different approach would be to follow the history of the table. You don't have to look very far back in Western history to find that the dining table was unknown in most households—just as it is in many contemporary non-Western settings now. The idea of a family grouped together in this formal manner, with the father in the most important position, is a late innovation, coming from elite culture and carrying a number of ideological notions of a proper domestic life. (In the next chapter, "Sharing a Meal," we will return to the question of what effect a table can have on people.) By interviewing different generations about the role of the table and changing table manners, it is possible to learn not to take present patterns for granted. There is also some rich material available in movies and soap operas where very different situations of family togetherness or conflicts around the table are depicted.

The three studies mentioned here open up a number of analytical entrances to the home, where the object is to describe and analyze both the material and sensual dimensions in homemaking. Hands-on methods are used to make the familiar strange. What they share is a kind of ethnography where the researcher is present in people's daily lives, walking through the rooms, talking to the occupants, and sometimes video recording, but always activating all the senses in order to capture the changing emotional atmosphere. Research becomes a physical activity, in motion close to where the action is.

These studies suggest not only methods to try but also questions to ask. They help us to look at the home as social and cultural processes rather than as stationary phenomena. They inspire us to examine how homes are created, maintained, and changed. Finally, they remind us never to ignore the seemingly trivial details when exploring everyday life.

TO AVOID THE PREDICTABLE

Our next step is to do informal interviews with some young people about how their experiences and feelings of home are produced or contested. In the beginning, the answers may be rather predictable, such as this one: "For me, home is the place where I feel safe, secure, and satisfied. It's my castle. It's also a place where I know that other people are caring for me."

One person after the other says that home is where they "feel at home," where they have their family and their important things, where they cook and eat, and sleep at nights. They close the door, live in peace, and are allowed to "be themselves." This last expression, "to be oneself," is a mystical phrase that often appears in these first interviews, for example, in this answer from a young woman:

> Home is calm and a haven. It's a place, a room, a sheltered spot, an atmosphere, a town, a country, a person, a bodily attitude. Home means to let go of everything on the outside, all murmurs and every sound, all the tensions and disguises you are carrying. You are just relaxing and being totally yourself, calm and comfortable. At home you may wear jogging pants and not bother about having a shower for two weeks, if that's what you want to do.

When the questions are too open and general ("What is a home for you?"), they illicit answers such as these. They may say something important about the thoughts and feelings the concept of home may arouse, but they hardly produce any new knowledge or provide surprising insights. They often echo the general public discourse on the home, ready-made clichés that are easy to use when asked. "Home" almost takes on a mythical quality.

Here we encounter a problem that is similar to the polarity the historian John Gillis (1996) points to in his study of family ideals. He writes about two ways in which people talk about families. On the one hand, there are the families they actually *live in*—all those relationships, routines, and emotions that one has to learn to manage; on the other, there are the families people *live with*, and the ideas about how a real family should be. The assumption is that families constantly compare themselves and their home with those of other families—in the media, in literature, and in real life. What kind of feelings do such comparisons produce? Vague guilt about not being good enough? Longings for a more perfect home? Or the feeling of being just right?

There might also be interesting contradictory ideas about the home. The classic talk of the contemporary home as this "sheltered spot" or "a haven in a heartless world" may hide the fact that home is also the place where you encounter the global world through the domestic media, whether through the TV in the sitting room or surfing the Internet in bed. But does all the talk about sheltered spots and "being yourself" contain anything worth considering? Yes, it provides a clue that leads us away from the self-evident—the home seems to be more about emotions, relations, and memories than just about a place for living. How, therefore, can we tackle such emotional dimensions?

CHOOSING METHODOLOGICAL ENTRANCES

What if we focus on the home as a place for different kinds of *events*, both those that are possible to observe and those that are more elusive, for example, habits, rituals, and performances? By asking people to describe such events—like morning routines, doing the weekly laundry, or watching a favorite evening show—you may hear them say something about relationships, conflicts, expectations, longings, and even secrets. When you ask about very concrete things and listen patiently, the answers may very well jump from one mental association to the next in unexpected ways.

Staying with down-to-earth matters, and the memories and emotions they raise, will also bring forward social variations of age, gender, and social background rather than sweeping statements. Instead of trying to find out what home is or what it signifies in general terms, we can zoom in on situations, actions, and memories, which may produce more surprising and wide-ranging answers.

In our search for new openings when studying the home, we have felt relatively free. But when writing a student essay, you do not have a large amount of time to spend on testing different methods. Even in more-extensive research, the researcher has to confront the problem of selecting certain roads to go down and ignoring others. In the following, we will look at this dilemma and argue for ways of choosing a topic. Again, the strategies mentioned could be used for almost any topic in the study of everyday life.

Selecting methodological entrances is like finding doors to open or windows to look through—apt metaphors when exploring homes. You will see different things, depending on which entry you take. This makes the choice of method and perspective important. You have to reflect on why you decide, for example, to make interviews, carry out observations, plan an informal survey, or surf discussions on the Internet. Each method will be able to answer certain questions and produce a special kind of knowledge.

But methodological awareness is not enough. You also have to think about analytical concepts and interpretive standpoints. You will get different results if you look at the home as a cultural system than if you explore it as a social arena or a transmitted tradition. Your study will go in one direction if you use a gender theory and in another if you use a class perspective—and in yet another if you try to combine them. Perhaps you employ the home as a laboratory for testing ideas or as material for studying other problems, such as the tensions between public and private. The selection of methodological entrances is always linked to theoretical perspectives.

NEW QUESTIONS AND SURPRISING ANSWERS

Let us try an informal survey. As in the previous chapter, on the importance of small things when moving in together, we decided to ask students to write down their experiences of the home, giving them different topics to consider. Through these simple exercises, we collected more than sixty accounts in a short time and thus created some material to work with.

The first task was to describe what it means to be "at home." The second was to describe one's home for a stranger from abroad. Both these topics turned out to generate rather trivial and predictable answers. In a couple of cases, however, there were things we had not thought of, such as:

> *When I have moved somewhere or traveled abroad, I used to bring the same detergent as my parents used. It's a scent that I recognize from my childhood and that makes me feel safe and secure. When my clothes and bedding smell as in the earlier years, I feel at home wherever I am staying.*

Fragrances as expressions of home feelings—this sensory dimension may be something to explore further, as Sarah Pink exemplified in her book. How does a home smell—in the kitchen, the bathroom, the wardrobe, or on the couch? How do different scents influence the experience of feeling at home or not feeling at home?

In another answer, a woman wrote that she had recently returned home after two years traveling as a backpacker. For her, the rucksack had been her "home." Now she had moved back into her apartment where all the familiar things made her feel at home. Then she remembers her childhood home that her mother left after a divorce.

> *My grandmother is sad because of that. She says that we, the grandchildren, don't have a real home any longer. In my father's house, I don't feel at home in spite of the fact that I have lived there for many years. In fact, I feel more at home in the house where my mother lives with her new husband. It's odd, because I have never stayed there for more than a couple of days.*

By choosing questions like these—or quite different ones—and trying them out with friends or in a quick Facebook survey, you have initiated your research and have some things to think about further.

RETURN TO THE PAST

One question that was very fruitful was asking people what they remembered about their home when they were, for example, seven years old. Try to travel back in time and find yourself walking around in this childhood space. Approaching the home as a site of memory really got people going and provided some rich and surprising material. How do middle-aged persons remember their teenage home? What could senior citizens relate about their living places during different life stages? This perspective was also tried in one of the case studies in Daniel Miller's book (2001: 75ff.), where the home of one older working-class woman was described as a private museum of memory, identity, and creative appropriation. She surrounded herself with all the things she loved, which evoked recollections of different homes in her life. You can ask people to take you on a walk through the rooms among objects that may function as a nostalgic shrine or a tiny link to a particular past.

Even many of the young students had already experienced several different homes and the memories from when they were seven years old are both concrete and vivid. Our specific question made them alert to the small details, just as we hoped.

> *I had a room with blue carpet. On the walls I had posters with the Spice Girls and the Backstreet Boys. My room was my own special place in our house. I played with my friends there. I collected my secrets there.*
>
> *In the kitchen daddy often cooked, mostly fish if I remember correctly. He had his office in one part of the house. Daddy's office was a forbidden place. But occasionally I was allowed to enter it and play Snoopy on his Mac.*
>
> *In the basement, I had six hamsters in the boiler room. Mom almost never went down there. She called my hamsters rats, which I can understand today. How many seven-year-old children have six hamsters in the basement?*
>
> *On Sundays, mom made breakfast and we watched Sailor Moon on channel four. I liked Sundays because then you were allowed to eat in front of the TV set.*

This little story illustrates several themes that also show up in many of the other twenty answers. They feature special rooms and places, routines and other activities, relationships and emotions. Our question got the students to travel in time and to reconstruct more or less nostalgic memories. It is the seven-year-old child's perspective that shapes the stories about the importance of parents, brothers, and sisters. It is the child that experiences the rules and the order at home, as well as the freedom to play and explore the surroundings. All this is captured through details: the colors and the patterns of the carpet in the bedroom, the house pets and the cuddly toys, books and films.

Most of the students choose to remember only nice things from the childhood home. There are few unpleasant memories. Perhaps an exercise like this one is not the right occasion to relate more traumatic experiences of violence and suffering. Neither are we told about any family secrets. When a trauma is disclosed in one of the stories, it is only briefly mentioned: "To be dragged out from under dad's desk to go to his new apartment. Not good. That didn't feel like home."

What is especially interesting in these stories is the degree of detail, which can be taken further. You could ask people to draw a map of their house or apartment, a method that is utilized by one of the researchers in Daniel Miller's book. If you separate it into different zones, how are the rooms and the nooks and crannies charged by memories and feelings? An emotional map of the home may show where irritations gather, or the spaces for happy togetherness or the creeping feelings of boredom. In what situations does sudden "home rage" invade the rooms? Emotions may be stored in kitchen cupboards or in a piece of furniture, harboring old resentments or blissful memories. What special rules were applied to the kitchen, the bathroom, or the bedroom? How was all this experienced by the seven-year-old child?

A LIFE-HISTORY PERSPECTIVE

After exploring such spontaneous images and memories, you need to limit your approach and get deeper into the material. The childhood interviews made us interested in a life-history perspective. What if we asked people to narrate their lives as homemakers? This is a restricted question that makes us concentrate on one specific theme and disregard others for a while.

The answers we received alerted us to how the meaning of home varies depending on the stage in one's life cycle, but there is a more important lesson to be learned here. Earlier experiences taught us to avoid opening up a broad life-history perspective. People may find it difficult or even provocative to be asked to "tell the story of their life." It is much easier to talk about "the kitchens in my life" or "homes I have lived in." Such a take tells a lot about one's life history, one's family life and social relationships. The "home" is a focal point for the degree of an individual's dependency on other people. It is also part of a narrative that touches on dramatic events, crucial changes, and strong emotions.

The life-history perspective is, moreover, about taking in different places in the world. Every home has a geographical dimension. You may move, for example, between countryside and urban surroundings, between countries, or from a poor neighborhood to a more affluent area (or the other way round). Why and how did this happen? How did taste, style, and habits change as a consequence of the movement?

When people talk about their different homes, their own life history follows as a shadow. When we step inside the apartments and houses that we are told about, we also open doors to different stages of life where people change between being children, teenagers, husbands or wives, parents, and senior citizens. In a way, walking around a home with a person can be like excavating a life; there are objects that operate as time machines, activating memories or coming to represent certain life stages.

A vaguer topic is brought up by a couple of questions that we come across in this connection. Is there some kind of continuity of feeling at home, even though people keep moving and setting up new living spaces? To what extent do you carry your home with you as you move? Such feelings may be hard to get at or put into words. A life of homemaking may be full of secrets and emotions. There will always be locked cupboards or dark closets with unknown contents that people are reluctant to remember or share.

THE STRANGE HOME

Another methodological entrance is to have people look at their own home as if they were a total stranger. This will be a different exploration from that of the life-history study. The point of choosing such a strategy is to experiment with the imagination as a tool for opening the eyes.

We asked a group of students to go home, open the door, and pretend that they had not been there before and that they had no idea who was living there. They should act as if they were explorers in a strange land and write down what they observed and experienced.

It is not easy to behave as real strangers in well-known surroundings. We recognize everything and identify ourselves with all these things that we have seen and used thousands of times. In spite of being trained ethnographers, we have to admit that we ourselves did not succeed very well in describing our couches, our dinner tables, or the paintings on the walls with "new eyes." Neither were we good at using our other senses to describe our homes as a strange place. How would the students handle this demanding task?

To our delight we found that the students took the exercise seriously and they returned with stories and descriptions that convincingly conveyed astonishment at the places that they were more than familiar with. They described how they were prying about, opening doors and closets, rummaging among the things and making guesses about what they all meant. Who lives here, how do they occupy themselves, and what are their interests? The titles of books and CDs were noted down, as well as the labels on perfume or bottles of shampoo in the bathroom. Home decorations and kitchen equipment were described. Did order or chaos prevail? What feelings did the things in the apartment convey and how did they make it into a special home?

To achieve this distance from their own home, several of the students used a particular trick. They wrote "I assume that . . ." or "I guess . . .," meaning that they assumed that it is a man or a woman, or a couple of people, who

Figure 3.2. **Differences in size and scale can often be an entry point into unexpected topics. Why are these men driving miniature vans? Why is the crowd watching them? (Richard Wilk)**

were living in the apartment. They guessed that the occupants were working or studying, that they liked to read certain things or listen to certain kinds of music, that they devoted their time to sports and athletics, to cooking, computer games, or artistic activities. Another trick in doing this is to describe things as if it is the first time that you are looking at them.

A few of the students wrote so credibly that it was difficult to understand that they really were in their own home. They also seemed to be sincerely surprised at how it all looked there and what kind of impressions and feelings it expressed:

> *The first thought that hits me when I step inside the yellow row house is that it looks very tidy and well organized. Everything is neat and proper. I can't find a single grain of dust or sand, not even on the floor in the hall where the shoes are lined up in perfect rows on the shelf.*

The observer walks like a detective from room to room and notes the shoe sizes and the drinking glasses in the kitchen that are arranged according to their color and volume. He opens the fridge and notices the perfect order even here; it is clean and no products are past their best-before date. A cookbook on the table has seven bookmarks in it, indicating that the cooking is planned weekly and that the diet is balanced. The dishes contain a lot of fruit and vegetables, no sweets or other futilities. A training schedule hangs on the fridge door. On the upper story, there are three more rooms that are described in detail. They express different orderings and tastes from the rooms below.

Afterward, at the seminar when the student talked about this exercise, he said that he had discovered several things in his own home that he had earlier hardly noticed and had not given any thought to. He was fascinated by the magic of concentrated observation and writing, how much he could see and think just by naming it.

In another story, the student forgets to keep a distance. She changes between being an insider and an outsider. She obviously shares an apartment with her little sister, and they have totally different habits concerning order and tidiness. So when she walks around in the apartment describing it meticulously as if she was a stranger, she cannot avoid putting the sister's things, like her hairgrips, underwear, and a cell-phone charger, in their right places. When she enters the bathroom she notices a wooden sculpture of a seagull in the window. It is a gift from their mother, a gift that the sisters, however, do not like very much. She surprises herself when she finds herself thinking that "if I lived here, I would have thrown the seagull away to let in more light." At the end of the observation exercise, she throws the sculpture in the garbage bin.

One of the purposes of an exercise like this is to train your capacity to observe familiar surroundings as if they were strange to you. One way to accomplish this is by using techniques of alienation, distancing yourself from the well-known—for example, by writing about it, or taking pictures. Then you may discover how the order of things is not as self-evident as it usually seems to be.

THE HOME AS AN ART INSTALLATION

Now it is time to try yet another methodological perspective, by asking what we can learn from contemporary artists. Art? Are you really allowed to use artistic methods in research? Our idea is that ethnographers and cultural researchers should be quite open-minded when it comes to experimenting with materials and perspectives. The main purpose is, as we have said, to produce surprising knowledge. Here, we may in fact have something to learn from art.

Artists are often good at distancing themselves from the self-evident, using all kinds of techniques of alienation. In one of his works, Robert Gober explores the idealized world of the needlepoint plaques, found in so many homes, that have the message: "Home is where the heart is." By twisting the message with the addition of a single word, he opens up a very different perception of what a home can be: "Home is where the heart is . . . broken." In his installation, a kicking leg breaks through the living room wall.

In a similar way, in her video "Semiotics of the Kitchen," Martha Rosler turns a docile domestic setting into something else. There she is, standing with an apron on in the middle of the kitchen solemnly presenting one harmless kitchen utensil after another but demonstrating with violent movements how each one can be turned into a weapon. Peaceful pans, whisks, and pestles are charged with new and threatening meanings.

Both Gober and Rosler remind us that the home is one of the most dangerous places. It is the most frequent arena for both mental and physical violence—between couples, young siblings, or parents and children. Another artist, Louise Bourgeois, illustrated this by building models and life-size replicas of her childhood home, which look rather like torture chambers or prison cells—there is no nostalgia here.

Still other artists have focused on the overflow of domestic stuff. In the installation "Unheimlich Maneuver," Klara Lidén stacked up all the belongings from her own apartment, turning them into a barricade of furniture, CDs, clothes, and tools. Objects take on new meanings as they are squashed together, her bike embracing the sofa cushions, toiletries mixed with books, underwear with repair tools. Somehow she also manages to capture the pent-up emotions squeezed together between the objects.

Artists like these are out to map the dark or hidden sides of home. Here, there is a connection with the ideas of the anthropologist Mary Douglas (1991), mentioned earlier. She reminds us that the home is very much a moral economy with its own rules. There is an entanglement of conventions and often incommensurable rights and duties. Questions of solidarity, fairness, and hierarchy are rarely talked of directly but may surface in conflicts over privacy and priorities, or in quarrels about routines.

Through such examples it may be possible to study domestic tensions, for example, between individual aspirations and activities and "the family or household good." There is a diffuse "we" often hovering in the background. Do "we" really need a new TV, a bigger house, or dessert for dinner? Looked at from this perspective, home is a site of negotiation, with constant wheeling and dealing, where the family or household members try to make different priorities and interests cohabit. Certainly, for many people, home can turn into a space that is claustrophobic and suffocating.

Without attempting to make sophisticated art installations, the ethnographer can be inspired by art projects that open up the potential for tackling such touchy issues. What if you ask people to choose one of their favorite possessions and place it next to something they had always wanted to throw away—or draw a map of the three worst conflict areas in the kitchen? You could also ask them to use grass, sticks, and stones to build a model of their bedroom. You could have them pick out ten blue objects and line them up in order of emotional significance. The point with such playful experiments is that you cannot predict where they will lead the investigation; they might open up new dimensions of domestic life.

THE IMPORTANCE OF DETAILS AND ACTIVITIES

In the previous chapter we discussed how trivial habits may disturb the most passionate relationship. Here, in this chapter, one can notice the difference between talking about the home in general statements and describing it through emotionally charged particulars—like the color of the carpet or hiding under the desk. The various approaches we have discussed show how crucial it is to ask your research questions in a manner that teases out other people's hidden thoughts and memories.

If you succeed with this, you will perhaps get some answers that show how the respondents seem to *discover* their experiences, and they don't just relate them. When they start talking or writing about their home, whether past or present, they probably do not know in advance what they are going to say. They begin with what comes to mind and then follow a path of association to continue the story, or stop to reflect on what they have said. For example, one student opened her presentation in this way: "When I was a child, my home was mainly constructed by rules, structures, and even independence."

Then she explained what this meant by talking about who made the decisions about each matter: what kind of rules and routines would prevail in each part of the home, and the social roles the parents and the three children would play in relation to each other. She describes herself as "the rebellious one," the person who challenged the rules and tested the patience of her parents while her sisters were more obedient. This could be an entry into a discussion of the home as a moral economy.

Again, it is the *life* in the home that is portrayed as the main topic, not the arrangement of furniture and other things. When the material objects are mentioned, they are something that has a function in this student's life. She does something with them.

It is the home *activities* that seem to be easiest to remember from childhood. Children play, quarrel, run around, and explore the basement and other spaces that have different functions and meanings for the seven-year-olds than they do for the adults. In the stories, the children alternate between being subordinated and adapting to the world of the grown-ups, and being free and creative. Those who lived in houses with yards, gardens, and garages transformed them into their own exciting playgrounds.

THE ADVANTAGES OF LIMITATION

Earlier we argued for the usefulness of the bricolage method, which means using several techniques to look for a number of different kinds of materials. In this chapter we have focused on one kind of material, people (mainly students) writing or talking about their experiences of home. Using such material as a starting point, we have then linked it to others.

The important thing here is to keep with one of the many topics and perspectives we have suggested in order not to drown in all kinds of interesting questions. Our aim was, as we declared, to explore the familiar phenomenon of "home" from unusual viewpoints—to make it strange and to discover something unexpected.

What did we learn? One lesson is to avoid eliciting general statements about how something is or should be, such as common attitudes and typical clichés. Try instead to observe or ask about people's experiences and activities. And in doing that, look for the concrete details and the seemingly insignificant things. There, you may find traces that lead to sudden discoveries. The point is to be prepared for seeing or hearing things that you had never dreamt of asking about.

Look for repeated actions and experiences in endless constellations. They may appear anywhere in the home, for example, in watered plants, messy cupboards, crumbs on the kitchen table, stacked telephone bills, or more-or-less-successful home-improvement projects. In the chaos of conflicting plans and desires, routines maintain some kind of order—which can be easily threatened. Secret coded messages and hints fly through the air, sometimes interrupted by outbursts of questions and complaints. Where's the remote control? How many times have I told you not to leave clothes on the floor? Isn't it about time someone took the trash out? Who keeps turning down the thermostat? The Californian ethnographic study mentioned earlier found that the door of the fridge, which worked as a message board and communication center, was a good place to begin an expedition into the exotic world of a home (Arnold et al. 2012).

Finally, simply writing about the familiar may, as we have said, be a method for becoming more attentive to the extraordinary when things are going on as usual. The written words create an analytical distance from what you describe and make you stop for a while and look again. The methodological secret in this way of exploring everyday life is to never think that you have exhausted the possibilities of surprising yourself or the reader with even the most trivial matters.

Such techniques can be applied to almost any kind of overfamiliar everyday topic or phenomenon. Instead of focusing on the home, what about exploring what's going on in a commuter bus doing its usual morning round, or an office cafeteria, or a supermarket setting? Again, the object of study may—as in the case of the home—actually be a means for getting at something else: the cultural organization of emotions and dreams, tensions between public and private, class difference, or gender issues.

Finally, how do you know that you are standing in front of an overfamiliar setting that needs to be made exotic or *unheimlich*? One way is when your first reaction is: "What can I say about this oh-so-well-known thing—probably nothing!" Begin by developing your study from that zero point, and be ready for some surprises.

4

SHARING A MEAL

One of the most difficult things in doing ethnography and cultural analysis is to see the cultural order in the mundane details of daily life. In our first chapters we have shown how you can accomplish this by doing an ethnographic exploration of everyday life at home—in your own home or in the homes of your acquaintances. In this chapter we will continue this exploration by focusing on one special and limited event at home—family meals.

Your personal experiences of eating together with other people can be compared to other people's meals, and this is a good place to start, because, among other things, you will discover a great deal of hidden variety and differences in what seems to be a simple and ordinary event. The facade of normality conceals much diversity. You will then look closer at the different stages of creating a meal, from cooking, through serving and eating, to disposal and cleanup. The closer you look at the meal, down to the level of how each person conveys food to their mouths, the more diversity and complexity you will find.

At a higher analytical level, meals can be doorways to understanding larger cultural themes like formality and informality, authority, and cultural capital, and they connect directly to issues of how morality and order are both made and violated in daily life. This brings class, politics, and gender into the discussion of everyday life. Meals also present an opportunity to think more deeply about cultural reproduction. What exactly do children learn from their early experiences of meals, and how does this lead to both change and continuity in culture? How can there be so much diversity in actual practices among families within a culture that is imagined as a homogenous unit?

TABLE MANNERS

One of the first sets of rules we are learning from birth, even before we learn to control our bowels, is how to eat, a task of almost endless complexity that keeps changing as we grow up. By the time we are five, we have learned the names of hundreds of foods and dishes, we have developed a set of likes and dislikes, and we have been told which foods are good for us and which are "bad," though we might already have our own ideas about those values. We know something about how to eat with others ("don't grab food from your brother's plate!") and what kinds of foods come first and last in a meal ("don't eat that until you finish your broccoli!"). What is truly amazing about all this training is that we are learning more than rules; we are learning moral values, and not just about how we should treat our family members. The values we learn eating with our family include basic things like generosity and sharing, discipline and respect for authority, and more abstract things like religion and politics.

The family table is a central site where we train to recognize these moral values and see how they are supposed to work. But at the same meal we also discover that there is a huge distance between the way things are supposed to be and the way things really happen. So, for example, we may realize that we are supposed to love and help our younger sister, but we may also feel like she is a greedy little brat who needs to be kicked under the table when she eats with her mouth open and makes slobbering noises.

We hear our parents tell us about good manners and show us foods they love, but we also hear them talk about the awful people they have to work with, or the horrible food prepared by their neighbors, and the kinds of people who eat disgusting things. As we hear about ideals, we are also learning that there is a clear difference between ideals (*norms* in the language of social science) and real life.

This distance between the real and the ideal is another crucially important part of everyday life. Usually when it is brought to our attention, for example, if the person next to us at dinner makes loud slobbering noises when he or she swallows the soup, we see it as a personal failing. "Where did you learn to eat, a pig sty?"

But from your point of view as a beginning ethnographer, you cannot just dismiss something like bad manners as a personal fault or a failure to follow the norms of a culture. Instead, if you really watch closely at meals and other social events, you will find that nobody sticks to the rules all the time. In most cases, it would be completely impossible because the rules and norms contradict each other, so if you follow one, you break another. So we are supposed to "stand up for ourselves" when attacked, but we are also supposed to "turn the other cheek" and not rise to the bait when we are teased or criticized. My older brother would get a bigger slice of pie because he was older and bigger, but then I (in this chapter, Richard Wilk) would have to give him half my soda, because we have to "share and share alike."

Figure 4.1.   While people are often attached to the ideal of the family dinner table, in everyday life eating and snacking go on all the time. How are gender and power expressed in this kind of eating? (ThinkStock)

The thin boundary between the real and the ideal is always worth exploring if you are interested in everyday life. A remarkable thing that happens in this zone is the flourishing of diversity. One of my favorite illustrations of how this works is in a paper written by an anthropologist/consumer research duo, Melanie Wallendorf and Eric Arnould (1991). They interviewed Americans in detail about the dishes that appeared at their family Thanksgiving dinner and found that almost everyone told them their dinner was "traditional" and normal, just like everyone else's. But when they looked at what was actually served at those normal traditional dinners, everyone had a different set of dishes! Families had unique dishes that were not on anyone else's menu ("pistachio fluff" is one that sticks in my mind) or some sort of special bread or a different kind of stuffing. Even the turkey was not universal.

So everyone has a clear sense or vision of a "normal, traditional" Thanksgiving dinner, and at the same time they have a very specific knowledge of real dinners that are quite different. And they mostly don't dwell on the difference, sometimes they actively hide it, because people don't like to think of themselves as hypocrites or liars. When differences threaten to come out in the open, people often agree with each other not to talk about it. And even stranger, they don't even have to talk about creating these "danger zones" and "taboo topics." Sometimes the "gag rule" has to be stated clearly—"nobody is going to talk about Grandma's denture noises tonight at this table."

But mostly there is a kind of unspoken agreement not to point out that nobody really likes the creamed okra that Grandma always brings to Thanksgiving. This is an example of what may be called the "ugly baby" rule. If someone asks you what you think of their hideously ugly baby, you do not have to be honest and say it looks like a reptile. You can be equally honest by saying something like "beautiful hair" or "what a strong grip!"

THE HIDDEN WORLD OF THE DINNER TABLE

Because we have all been brought up eating meals, we have all the tools we need to do some research on the invisible culture of the family meal. Our own experience becomes a measuring stick that we can use to find and describe different norms and practices. Here is a simple example that you can try with anyone you happen to be sitting next to in class or on a train.

Imagine you have just been served a plate with two sausages, some mashed potatoes, a large spoonful of canned green peas, and some nice brown gravy in a small side dish. What condiments, like mustard or mayonnaise, would you want to add to this meal? How do you hold the knife and fork, and what do you do with each one? What do you eat first? Do you start with your favorite thing, and then your next favorite, or do you eat a little bit of each thing and then go on to the rest? Or do you mix some of the things together on the plate, or on your fork, or do you keep everything separate? How would you eat the gravy? Do you pour it on the potatoes, or do you dip the sausage in it?

Now give the same imaginary plate of food to the person sitting next to you and ask him or her the same series of questions. Even though you may have been brought up in the same town and share culture, you are going to find that there is no single stereotyped rule that everyone follows in eating the same plate of food. Some of those ways are going to be patterned by major social differences like gender or class. Women, in most of Europe and North America, are expected to eat more carefully and slowly than men; taking smaller bites seems "dainty."

Older people also tend to eat more slowly with less mixing. I was taught by my parents in subtle ways that it was disgusting to mix things together into a mess on the plate and then eat it down in big mixed bites; only uneducated and crude people slop up food like animals.

This example of what to eat first makes an important broader point. If you dig deep enough, you will always find that a moral value is connected with the way people consume things, from sausages to wedding rings. When you see people acting differently, you may find that you have a lower opinion of them, and some differences may make you feel disgusted, or they strike you as simply wrong. "Really? Gravy on peas!"

In daily life, most of the details of eating are acted out unconsciously without discussion; it is up to the ethnographer to elicit and provoke people to state the more general principles, or to observe contradictions and bring them to notice. A good example of how minor differences in meal practices can reveal larger and more serious social distinctions is given by the ethnologist Anders Linde-Laursen (1993) in his paper "The Nationalization of Trivialities." He visited kitchens to see how Danish and Swedish families wash the dirty dishes after a meal. These households were separated by only a few kilometers of water; they are now spanned by the Oresund Bridge, which physically connects the two countries.

On the Swedish side, dishes are rinsed, washed in hot, soapy water, rinsed again, and then set to dry in a rack. This is, according to the Swedish Domestic Research Institute, the "most rational and hygienic" way to wash dishes (of course before dishwashers became common). On the Danish side, dishes are rinsed, washed in hot, soapy water, stacked in a drainer and then wiped dry with a small towel. The Danes also think their way of doing dishes is rational and hygienic, as well as thrifty (saving water). If you confront them, both Danes and Swedes will probably say that their way is the right way. They may even be disgusted by the "other" way and tell you that the others do it wrong because of a national quality like fussiness or carelessness.

Once you start digging into the ways people structure their meals, you will find no end to the differences, to the point where no two meals are ever really alike. After all, you never eat exactly the same food twice. In my experience, people have no trouble talking about these differences, and once people understand what you want to know, they are happy to give you many intimate details. The exceptions tend to be people who may have grown up in great wealth or poverty, which may be embarrassing, or in an abusive situation that made mealtimes disturbing and painful to recall and recount. Even then, people are often very willing to talk, though it can be easier to start off with their best family meal instead of asking about meals in general.

The real problem is not finding differences between the people you talk to but figuring out whether they are personal or if they are connected to larger social categories like gender, class, wealth, age, ethnicity, or nationality. To answer those questions, you will need to interview a larger sample. Starting with one friend will give you confidence and open your eyes to distinctions you have not seen before. Expanding to a few more diverse people can give you some ideas about the range of variations out there. Maybe some people don't use knives to cut up their sausages and, instead, spear them with a fork and hold them up to take bites. Or perhaps you will find someone who doesn't eat sausages at all. Just recording and documenting how people eat has value in itself—our knowledge of daily life is still so limited and imperfect that you can add to what we know by simply describing behavior and explaining how norms (what people think they should be doing) are different from behavior (what they actually do).

From this small sample, you can then form some ideas about what patterns you might find. For example, you may find enough to make you think that maybe the order in which women are eating the items on their plate is different from that of the men's. Then you might choose to set up interviews, half with men and half with women, with the idea of comparing the two groups to see if your intuition (hypothesis) is correct. Or if you are interested in married and unmarried couples, you might choose to divide your interviews into three groups—married, unmarried living together, and unmarried not living together.

One good general rule of thumb in setting up interviews about a mundane everyday topic is to look for situations where the flow of everyday activity is disrupted. For example, people interested in studying the invisible rules that structure the way couples handle money find that when relationships come apart in a breakup or divorce, those assumptions and rules suddenly become visible. People state the beliefs and values that were felt but rarely voiced. The same kinds of issues often arise when couples first live together and the rules and habits have not been set yet.

FORMING A FAMILY MEAL

As already said, many people also have happy memories of family meals, or an ideal of what that dinner is supposed to look like. In our mind's eye, we can see the family passing food, smiling, exchanging news about their day, and sharing in one of life's most basic comforts. Yet, I recently interviewed a young man who described his dysfunctional family by talking about how horrible it was to eat with his divorced father and new stepmother. He said his father watched his every move and criticized his posture, his table manners, and the way he chewed his food. He had to stay at the table, listening to his father's endless bragging until he was excused, and then he had to clean up the kitchen and do the dishes by himself, as a retaliation for bad grades at school. Yet, he said that today, after escaping to college where he could have his own life, he loved preparing and eating meals with his close friends in a cooperative house.

None of us just reproduces the culture we get from our parents; we take things from our past and reuse them in new ways. We decide to make things different in our own lives, to keep some of the values and ideas we got from our own family, but we reject others and try to "fix them" in our own life. So growing up in a family formed by divorce may make us determined to have a stable relationship. But we also might find that we have habits and attitudes we are not even aware of that are undercutting a relationship, pushing us slowly into divorce despite our best intentions. We humans are a peculiar mixture of smart and stupid, sensitivity and cloddish ignorance about our own behavior. Sometimes we are calculating and thoughtful, and other times we just follow our habits or emotions and do stupid things even when we are aware that they are making things worse.

To show how everyone struggles to create something new out of the things passed on to them by earlier generations, I will use my own family, the social group I have studied most intensively. Autoethnography is not always the best place to *start* looking at something like family meals. In this case, my ethnographic studies of other people's families helped me a lot in figuring out more about my own. The study of everyday life often has this reflexive nature, where our own life experience helps us understand other people, and what we learn from others reflects back on our own personal life.

First, some background. I am a Jewish Yankee son of a writer and an artist, with an older brother and a younger sister. Like many anthropologists, I come from a family that moved often from place to place, including suburban Connecticut, Beverly Hills (California), and the center of London. When you are always the "new kid" at school, you have to learn to figure out how to fit in very quickly. But I never realized how different my own family's customs and habits were until I moved in with a girlfriend in college; and I discovered even more differences when I got married and had a child of my own.

My wife Anne Pyburn is also an anthropologist, a fourth-generation Texan whose grandfather was a roustabout in the oil fields, while her father was a biologist who took his family off for summers in Mexico and Colombia. When the two of us met in a mosquito-infested swamp in Belize, we were both thirty-five, old enough to have developed our own ideas about how to run a household. Our first years of marriage were full of collisions between her way and my way. Both of us are stubborn and used to being in charge. Anne managed a crew of some thirty students and archaeologists in a jungle camp every year, so she knows how to give orders. Still, over the years, we gradually blended things together to make "our way" of keeping house. But several difficult issues remained, and a constant problem was conflict over serving meals.

We had terrible arguments whenever we invited people over for dinner, and by the time people arrived, we were often furious with each other. I got mad because I wanted Anne to focus on the menu, the ingredients, and the recipes, but she was focused on how the house looked, how the table was set, and having lots of drinks and snacks out where people could graze before dinner. She wanted a table beautifully set with a tablecloth, place setting, wine and water glasses, candles and flowers. The actual food was not as important as the display—bowls and platters heaped with generous amounts, with extra bread and gravy ready at hand. I have always been more concerned with the menu and the ingredients. I want to present something unusual or fancy for a main course, with some familiar side dishes, and I want to use fresh local ingredients as much as possible. As a frugal chef, I don't like to waste anything, and I want to recycle containers and compost anything I cannot use.

So why can't we just work together in our own domains and have peace and harmony at the table? In our first years of marriage, we sometimes got so angry that we could barely look at each other when the guests finally arrived. It took us a long time to recognize that our clashes were caused by our expectations, by the ways we had been brought up with very different kinds of meanings attached to meals. We had very dissimilar ideas about the way people should care for each other and the social and moral meanings of food.

POWER AT THE TABLE

When I was growing up, my father often set the table, while my mother dominated the kitchen. When the meal was ready, she stood over the stove, and the family trooped in carrying their plates, holding them out to be filled. You could ask for a little more or less of something, but it took a good argument to refuse one of her dishes. If you wanted seconds, you went to get it yourself, though there might not be much left in the pan. Sometimes she kept cooking right through part of the dinner, especially something like potato pancakes that should be served freshly cooked. Then she would bring the pan into the dining room to serve directly onto our plates.

Cooking delicious food, serving us and being in control were her interpretations of how to be a good Jewish mother, something she had learned from her own mother and grandmother. My father, on the other hand, was the disciplinarian—he was in charge of making sure we ate our food, stopped kicking under the table, and asked to be excused before we could leave. He was the one to check our hands to make sure we washed them before dinner. But there was not much ceremony about the dinner; you ate as soon as you sat down, but when we were children we did have to ask to be excused from the table before running off.

Anne was never very comfortable eating with my family. My mother could be manipulative and ungenerous with her children's spouses, while, at the same time, she doted on her grandchildren and gave them everything they wanted. Even when my mother served a big holiday meal and put platters of food out on the table, Anne was uncomfortable with the way people grabbed things or asked people to pass them in a kind of random assault on the food, eating and talking loudly.

The way my family ate always seemed perfectly normal to me, but after Anne complained a few times, I began to see how the way my mother served food was rarely fair. She would sometimes save you your favorite piece of chicken, or she might give you the back and neck. Sometimes her in-laws got less food than her children, and there was no arguing with her decisions. There was one famous dinner where we all ate bloody rabbit because we were all afraid to tell her it was not fully cooked. There could be all kinds of messages in each ambiguous portion. Did she give you a small piece of meat because she thinks you're too fat? Is she waiting for you to ask for more so she can criticize you later? My mother's way of serving was a lesson in the close connection between food and power in the family.

My mother's cooking sent other messages, too. As an active artist and businesswoman, she was no housewife, so she did not make a lot of elaborate or complicated dishes. At the same time, she was a well-traveled gourmet who attended cooking school in Paris in her youth, so she liked to experiment with ethnic food. Her cooking said she loved cultural diversity and quality, but not ostentatious luxury. Her parents had escaped grinding poverty in the slums of New York, and this rise from hunger gave food some very complicated and conflicted meanings to her generation. Jews who lived through World War II are especially aware of how easy it is to lose everything and fall back into poverty, or worse. The moral lesson I learned from her table was that food is precious and never to be wasted, but it should also be a source of novelty and pleasure. We may be well-off, but we remember our roots, so we don't waste.

My memories of meals are all tinged with sadness now that both of my parents have gone. I did not realize just how peculiar my own family dinners were until I had a contrasting example for comparison. Anne learned to eat at a table surrounded by abundance. Instead of loading plates in the kitchen, her mother put all the food out on the table on platters, on boards, in bowls, gravy dishes, and saucers before calling people in to eat. The first part of the meal was devoted to an elaborate round of passing and helping, made more complicated by a forest of pitchers, utensils, and condiments. The meal was constantly interrupted by requests to pass this and that, and occasional trips back to the kitchen to refill even half-empty serving dishes. Nobody touched their food until everyone was seated and ready to start.

There were always abundant leftovers. During an extended holiday or family visit the refrigerator and freezer got so full of Tupperware, bowls, jars, and bags that it threatened to topple out when the door was opened. Serving and storing the meal required an enormous supply of cutlery and dishware, some of it family heirlooms that had to be hand washed and dried instead of going into the dishwasher.

My mother-in-law had nothing like my mother's constant control and supervision over the meal, but there was still an elaborate and subtle politics to serving food from platter to plate. You didn't want to seem greedy, so it was best to take less than you wanted and leave large or choice pieces for someone else. You had to take at least a little bit of everything to show your appreciation, and you didn't want it to look like you don't like the food.

Then there was always a mock argument between cook and guest. The cook would say something like, "I knew you would like the potatoes! They're my special recipe. Have some more." The diner might say something like, "Oh they were wonderful, but I am absolutely stuffed." The cook could continue to press potatoes again, and the diner either gives in or says something like, "I am saving myself for your wonderful pie."

This constant passing of food made me feel pressured to eat more than I wanted, as if I wasn't fat enough already. It also felt like the cook was fishing for compliments, forcing people to say they liked the food, even when they barely gagged it down. Unexpectedly, my experience living in small Mayan villages in Central America helped me to deal with my unease at my mother-in-law's table. The ritual of offering and refusing of food is a lot like the way Mayan villagers went about finding someone to serve as the village *Alcalde*—mayor—every year. The elders would meet and talk things over, and pick a candidate who could do the job. The thing is that being Alcalde is difficult and time consuming and may get a man involved in angry disputes over money, marriage, or property. So most people don't really want to do it, but they feel an obligation, and men know that they have to serve a term as Alcalde to become a respected elder.

So just like my mother-in-law offering me more potatoes, the elders go to the man's house, and they try to persuade him to take the job. They tell him everyone respects him, and it is his duty to the community, while he says he's not worthy, the burden of the job is too great, and he has to take care of his sick daughter. The elders beg, and he continues to refuse. A few days later they come back and ask again, longer and louder, saying that there is nobody else who could do the job as well, but usually he makes excuses and refuses again. Only a very determined man can say no a third time, and he'd better have a really good reason (no, I cannot eat another bite!).

Even though this little ritual looks like a formality, the elaborate conversation does some very important things. It reminds the candidate that the office of Alcalde is an important gift that carries a burden. The prospective mayor's sincere refusals reassure the village that they are not giving this gift to someone who is greedy for power, or will take the job lightly. At the same time, if he really does want to be Alcalde, the process helps make it look like he is really doing everyone a favor by giving in.

My mother-in-law's pressure to eat another spoonful of green-bean casserole works exactly the same way. Politeness covers the possibilities of greed, envy, and distaste like a blanket. This is the essence of American "southern hospitality," which northerners so often can't understand. You can't just say "no thanks" and end it there. Now I see that it is motivated by a real generosity; it's an effort to make everyone comfortable by making sure nobody looks greedy or hateful, even if they are. It expresses love by gracefully concealing other more difficult emotions.

CLASS AND FAMILY HISTORY

Understanding the "hidden transcript" of power at the table has helped me relax and accept Anne's way of serving meals, but wasting food still bothers me, even though I know it's a class issue. Unlike my folks, the children of the generation escaping poverty, Anne's parents were born poor and reached the middle class through hard work and education. Her dad was a terribly underpaid college professor, the first person in his family ever to go to college. In the hard times of his childhood in the Great Depression, there wasn't always enough on the table, so a groaning board of plates piled high with steaks, greens, and potatoes really meant something later in life.

The Pyburns' choice of what food to put on the table also tells a lot about their family histories. Abundance had a special meaning for the hearty German and English Protestant settlers of East Texas, who mostly came from poor peasant families. Fine and fancy dishes are treated with some suspicion. This democratic streak drives a lot of criticism of people who might appear to be getting above themselves and "putting on airs." Anne's parents always had to prove that while they were doing well, they didn't consider themselves superior, and that can be a tricky business. Their mealtime said something like, "We might not be fancy folk, but we can put out a big spread of good plain food."

I don't think anyone who lived through the Great Depression in poverty ever really forgot. That's one reason why we can't throw away all the mountains of food left over after a big meal at my mother-in-law's house. Most of it is carefully stored for a few weeks and gradually forgotten in the back of the fridge, only to be thrown away when it is spoiled. She has a hard time throwing away old jars, wrapping paper, greeting cards, and plastic containers, too. I don't think this habit is simply about the fear of losing everything again. Instead, the things you save are little tokens of virtue. In a world where just about everything is now temporary and disposable, keeping old jars, tins, and containers is a kind of protest, standing in the path of unwelcome progress by blocking the flow, one mason jar at a time.

Anne and I have both inherited a morality of thrift from our parents, but we express it in different ways. If she sees a jar of the right size and shape, she puts it in the dishwasher. Anne knows we don't need more containers, but it still feels right somehow. When I find them, I take them out and put them in the recycling bin—this is my way to convert waste into virtue. By recycling things I don't have to keep them, but I don't have to throw them away either. I like going to the recycling center, which is always full of virtuous people being thrifty in the modern way that allows us the joys of consuming without guilt. In Anne's family saving things was private, even a little furtive, a hangover from bad days better forgotten. In mine, not wasting was a matter of pride and self-control, done very much in public to demonstrate virtue. So she saves jars in the cupboard, and I fill the garage with recycling.

I am sure that Anne and I could have avoided a lot of conflict over serving dinner if we just accepted our parents' gender roles. Like her mother and my mother, she would run the kitchen and serve the meals, and I would eat and then help with the cleanup, and that would be that. I never saw Anne's father so much as boil water, and my father wasn't even happy in the traditional male role as master of the barbeque. Because Anne and I are committed to equality in every part of our relationship, we have had to negotiate everything from who gets up to change the baby to who gets to pick the next fieldwork site, and who will be senior author on our next paper together.

But while this makes us unusual in some respects, we are completely typical in others. All families have their histories, lore, and traditions, and every generation has conflicts over class, cultural difference, and family roles that get worked out at the dinner table. None of us can escape our roots and early learning, and later in life we have to learn to deal with the habits and expectations our parents gave us. The drama around the table is often subtle or even hidden, but I suspect that for many people, it is much more important and sometimes more fulfilling than the food itself. For the exact same reason, there are others who hate family meals, and I am sure there are many couples who find themselves arguing over seemingly insignificant minute details like where the fork should go and when to toss the salad.

DOING MEALTIME ETHNOGRAPHY

A good way to enter into the meaning of everyday events is to participate, taking note of things that seem "charged" with meaning, objects or events that

Figure 4.2. All over the world, there are wallpaper images like this one, showing the perfect family dinner, backdrop to the more chaotic realities of domestic meals. (Print from the 1950s; photo: Orvar Löfgren)

seem out of place, moments of tension, or general hilarity. Then talk to two or three of the participants afterward. What did Uncle Henry really mean when he said your mother's food always left him feeling overstuffed like a goose? Why did the group make such a fuss over your sister not eating her food? Why did the topic of conversation end so suddenly when someone brought up the next presidential election? What old hurts and arguments were causing such tension at one point in the meal? It is up to you to decide which kinds of topics you want to pursue. Are you more interested in gender issues, generational changes, and attitudes toward new technologies? What happens to a Christmas dinner when everyone is texting their friends instead of talking to each other?

Daily routines are always cultural assertions of order, barriers that we use to keep out the chaos of having to make millions of decisions just to get through the day. Routines often divide good and bad behavior and, thereby, set moral boundaries. The task of anyone studying everyday life is to connect the topic of research to other people's work, to make it appeal to a wide audience of people who are thinking about other things. It is your task as a researcher to connect what you find interesting with broader issues, helping others to see how your research is relevant to what they are doing.

As we have already mentioned, ethnography and cultural analysis do two things very effectively. They can make familiar, comforting things suddenly seem strange and exotic, or turn the direction around to show how something exotic and strange is really easy to understand. Meals provide opportunities to make both kinds of movement. The simple routine of placing food out on the table is laden with meanings that are usually opaque to those around the table. They normally emerge in social settings where we are guests or partners in preparing, consuming, and cleaning up after meals.

Anyone who shares a kitchen or dining space with another person has to face different assumptions and unconscious habits gained through a lifetime of experience. For example, if you have friends living in student housing where they share kitchen space, take a look in the refrigerator. If the milk and eggs have labels on them saying whom they belong to, you can be sure the room-mates have not figured out how to share meals in a family-like way. The people living there should be able to explain their differences very clearly, since they have to deal with conflicts every day. In functioning families, those same differences may be deeply concealed and difficult to elicit. You may have to contrast two different families or get people to tell stories about how their meals today are different from those of their childhood.

Another way to penetrate the appearances and habits that allow people to navigate the complexity of everyday life is to explore the differences between the real and the ideal. In family meals, these differences are especially clear because most ideal "normative" meals are so far from the reality of meals grabbed while driving a car, watching television, or catching up with Facebook. You might get people to contrast their real meals with the ones they have during holidays; or ask them to describe their best and worst meals in the last few weeks. The key is to keep at least part of the focus on the present day or the very recent past, when specific events ("dinner last Friday") can be contrasted with timeless and generalized ideals ("having a dinner party"). You can do a similar form of "unpacking" with many other activities in everyday life, from getting dressed in the morning to managing the use of the TV remote control.

A good practical exercise in mealtime ethnography is to turn yourself into the observer at your own family or group meals and other celebratory events that involve food and drink, like tailgating, birthdays, and Valentine's Day. Often there are ghosts of past arguments, broken relationships, or family incidents that are lying beneath small avoidances, muttered comments, or the absence of some expected item, like the candles on top of a birthday cake. Try to look at the balance between individuality and conformity—what sociologist Georg

Simmel (1910) calls "fitting in" and "standing out," one of the key conflicts in consumer culture. How is the event different from what has become "typical"? In what ways does it conform? Pay attention to when people talk and when they are silent, and to who leads the conversation. When does the whole group participate, and when does it break up into smaller groups?

MEALS AS MODELS

The example of the family meal shows you several different strategies for finding broader relevance and connections with major issues in social science. Everyone eats, but few people ever step back and think seriously about their routines and expectations. By paying attention to details and variations, you can surprise people by showing them things they never expected about their daily routines. This provides an opening for bringing up issues of gender, class, and power that are normally hidden from view or systematically ignored because of their disruptive potential.

It is also important to notice the way discourse about the family falls into familiar patterns, often based on the genre that could be called "the death of the family." Every generation seems to believe that the family is about to disappear, that families in the past were more harmonious or cohesive. These laments usually come with a putative cause, like too much listening to the radio, lack of respect for elders, or some kind of social media. How can you eat and tweet at the same time? And then there is a prescription: parents must spend more time with their children, children need to spend more time at the dinner table, or help more often with preparation and cleanup. This kind of complaint has been heard during the whole history of recent family life, creating a nostalgic "then" or a golden age when families stuck together.

These ideas about what a proper family should look like are themselves worth investigating, for they tell a great deal about the things people value and how they perceive cultural and technological change. They are also charged with political meanings. In truth, we really do not know very much about how politics are related to family life and daily meals. This is a research frontier where every student can explore and make new discoveries. One of the key insights we offer in this book is that everyday life is full of unexplored areas, topics as unknown as the deep sea or outer space. My example of the dinner table is hardly exhaustive or definitive—rather than as a finished story, it should be taken as an invitation to a different kind of feast.

5

DO YOU REMEMBER FACEBOOK?

Offline for a week, without mobile, laptop, or the Internet—that shouldn't be so hard. This is what the journalist Hanna Fahl thought, and inspired by other experiments of nondigital living (see Maushart 2010, for example), she begins her trial. But it doesn't work at all. She discovers straightaway how much she has outsourced to digital technology: phone numbers, meeting times, to-do lists, itineraries, music titles—everything she has stopped remembering and just clicks her way into. She feels like she is losing control of her everyday life, which begins to get complicated with everything moving infuriatingly slowly. The people she tells about her experiment of an Internet-free week are enthusiastic: "Sounds great, just like a dream!" Hanna wants to punch the next person who says that in the face. She can hardly wait for the week to end. She longs for the Net, to just click in and out of cyberspace. "I miss the external hard drive for my brain."

EXPLORING MEDIA IN EVERYDAY LIFE

In the three earlier chapters, the home as a field of activity was in focus. Now we will use the home as a platform for reaching out into the world, by looking at the role of media and home electronics in everyday life.

A well-worn cliché is that new media are continually revolutionizing everyday life, but what about turning the argument around: how does everyday life revolutionize new media? What happens when a video camera or a smartphone is introduced in domestic lives and how do the sofa, the kitchen sink, or the children's toys interact with our media use? People begin to experiment and combine new gadgets with other activities in ways that may drastically change technology and that even may hijack it from its intended use.

When the videocassette recorder (the VCR) was introduced it was seen as a research tool and a medium for artists. It didn't take long for it to result in a rapidly expanding global infrastructure of new lending "libraries." Everywhere, small video rental stores could be found where local families or teenagers went to get a couple of movies, some soft drinks, and popcorn for the ritual of Saturday night togetherness.

When the cell phone was new, no one foresaw that this tool for business-people would be taken over by teenagers, who turned it into a multitasking tool that continually found new uses. A visit to the website www.deadmedia .org will remind you of all the media that never made it or died an early death, often because they did not resonate with everyday needs and routines.

This chapter, then, is about doing media ethnography. The main questions are what media do to people and what people do to media. How do they learn about new technology and forget old ones? How do they acquire media skills in ways that make these competences sink into the body and often become imperceptible? Again, we are faced with the task of interviewing people about knowledge they take for granted and, perhaps, they are not even able to verbalize.

At home there is an overflow of gadgets, cords, remote controls, and used batteries, creating domestic "mediascapes" (Appadurai 1996) that are accused sometimes of taking over people's lives. They produce a number of emotional reactions when they refuse to work, are wrongly programmed, feel irritating or unfashionable—or simply just go into hiding. "Has anybody seen my cell-phone charger?" is a common cry. Some technologies blend into the everyday in ways that no longer make them seem like media, like the post-it note on the fridge door or the piped muzak at the mall.

A standard way for doing a media-use project is to ask people about their media experiences—but why not try another tactic: looking at the life histories of objects. This focus is developed in a classic paper, by the anthropologist Igor Kopytoff (1986) that outlines a project on the life cycle of things, a journey from brand new to junk. His own example follows the life history of a car in an African city as it moves between owners and ends up as scrap metal. Kopytoff is interested in the interaction between users and commodities in the different stages of ageing. Such a perspective can easily be taken into the world of domestic media, for example, the life history of a game console, a TV set, or a cell phone.

I (in this chapter, Orvar Löfgren) choose to make a trip to the basement, to look for stuff rather than words. Down there, I inspect the media burial grounds of dusty photo albums, shoe boxes full of snapshots, music and video cassettes, old cameras, Nintendo games, and stacks of vinyl records. In most homes, you will find collections like this, if not in the basement, then maybe in a couple of boxes stashed in the back of a wardrobe. It might be piles of old comic books, CDs and photos, yesterday's camera, just abandoned files on the hard disc, or old favorite music lists on the cell phone that have never been erased. What kind of stuff is this? A family archive, a media burial site, or just forgotten junk? Questions like this may be useful when it is time to interview people.

Down in the basement, I am reminded of how fast things age; the gadget that now looks hopelessly out of date was once an exciting innovation, full of promises for the future. Upstairs there is all the trendy stuff waiting to go through the same kind of ageing process. Soon much of what is used right now will turn into cultural history. "Does anyone remember Facebook or Twitter?"

BEGINNING AT THE END

Where to go after the basement? Reading Kopytoff's discussion about the life cycle of things, I opt for a visit to two end destinations: a local recycling station and a thrift store.

At my local recycling station, people are supposed to sort their trash into different containers, and the crew at the station supervises this process and prevents people from reclaiming other visitors' junk. The final destination is industrial recycling only. As a concession to the difficulties of letting go of things, there is, however, a shed in which objects can be placed for reselling by a charity organization.

There is a special recycling space for electronics. In the containers, I see car radios, cassette players, an abundance of speakers in all sizes and shapes, old telephones, and a wealth of computer equipment. All this waste is a highly visible reminder of the short life span of many media products, the result of successful marketing of the need for constant upgrading.

Watching people throw away dead media at the recycling station, I can sense the mixed feelings. Seeing the mess of mutilated things crammed into the containers, some people hesitate before they let go of their belongings. "Maybe I should consider giving this telephone or computer to the charity thrift shed next door?" But on that door is a scribbled note: "We don't accept old electronics." Dead media are not welcome here. The difficulties of recycling media stuff have led to export systems, sometimes thinly disguised as developmental help to Third World countries. Some ethnographers have followed media objects as they travel to cities such as Lagos in Nigeria and Guiyu in China where old computers and television sets pile up (Parks 2006).

My next stop is the local thrift store, which has a special section for home electronics. Walking along the overcrowded shelves is like following the history of media since the 1960s. There are elegant radio gramophones, typewriters, transistor radios, hi-fi stations, game consoles, and cell phones. Add to this list a number of gadgets that are hard to identify—what were they used for?

Back home from the recycling station and the thrift store, I have brought with me photos and field notes that feed into new questions and possible directions for upcoming interviews. I could have chosen other sites to visit, but the important thing was to get away from the desk and see media in new settings.

One potential topic concerns the dynamics of fashion in the life cycle of domestic media. The box of yesterday's assorted cell phones at the thrift store illustrates a short life span, whereas the box next to it containing yesterday's trendy plastic covers for the telephones radiates an even stronger aura of rapid fashion changes. Much of the stuff thrown into the bins at the recycling station still worked. Home electronics rarely get worn out; they are discarded because they feel unfashionable or outdated. This theme of cultural rather than physical wear and tear is worth pursuing. All of a sudden you look at a computer game, a camera, or a home page with new eyes—it now seems hopelessly out of date. Time to let go! How does this happen, and why is it that some stuff ages more rapidly than others?

Interviewing people about how they have grown tired of belongings opens up a number of major issues. In the global media industries, enormous investments are made to shorten the life span of commodities. In the United States, the average life span of a black-and-white TV bought in 1979 was twelve years. In 2013, for a flat-screen TV, it was five years and for a cell phone, twenty-one months.

Marketers, designers, and technicians work hard to make objects age more rapidly, offering constant updates. Yesterday's graphics or design seems tired in comparison with the new offers. How do such campaigns of persuasion influence everyday consumption?

The reason for beginning with stuff rather than people is not only to create new interview questions but also to develop dialogues between people and their possessions. When you ask them to take a trip to the basement, or come along for a ride to the thrift store, a different kind of interview situation emerges. Something happens when they stand in front of actual objects and start handling them. Old memories and skills may come up to the surface, like turning the knobs of an old radio, maneuvering between different stations, or using your index finger to dial a phone number. It is possible to discuss what it is that makes this very cell phone feel outdated or what memories are prompted by the jingle of an early Nintendo game. The more senses that are brought into action, the sharper the observations become. Emotions also come into play. Does an old media piece produce a giggle, a shrug, or a nostalgic memory?

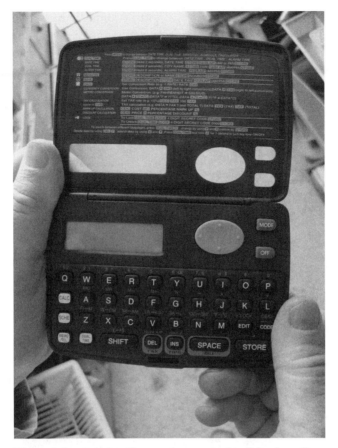

Figure 5.1. Another flea market example of dead media. Nobody remembers what it was used for. (It turns out to be a short-lived personal planner from the 1990s.) (Richard Wilk)

A man standing among the boxes of his old cassette-tape mixes down in the basement reflects:

I have put a bit of my soul into these mixes. I rarely play them, but it is fun to know that they still exist somewhere. I feel that the day will come when I am motivated to check out what I have kept. Opening such a box of tapes, you are just caught up. You just have to listen and then all the memories come back. Directly.

This man is also reminded of what Elizabeth Shove et al. (2012) call the "fossilization of objects." Down in the basement, there are media that nobody knows how to use or operate any longer. Looking into his boxes of old tapes, the labels with "Cr02," "Metafine," "Chrome," or "Dolby C" on them have lost their meaning.

Interviewing people about the life cycles of their old and new media and electronics may also highlight different kinds of trajectories. Some things get a second life as kitsch, retro objects, or collector's items. There is a striking selection here. How come old juke boxes, computer games, and cameras become cherished collector's items, but not computer printers or answering machines? There are studies of collector subcultures, collectors of old vinyl records and hi-fi, for example—subcultures that tend to be heavily gendered.

So far, a battery of potential research and interview questions has been suggested. What about choosing informants? Everybody is the media expert of their own everyday life, so there are plenty of informants to choose from. If the aim is to look at generational changes, one can compare one's own experiences with that of two very different age groups. Sit down with a seventy-year-old and a five-year-old and find out how they handle the same tool, an iPad perhaps. You may also ask people to do a media-use diary of a typical day—it might turn out to be quite a task. (In 2013, the average American owner turned to her smartphone more than 150 times a day.)

ANALOG AND DIGITAL LIVING

The next step is to widen the perspective from the history of objects to their use. How have people learned to handle new technologies that later became established, from TV sets to smartphones? I looked at some older studies and interview materials where people narrated their life with domestic media in the second half of the twentieth century. What was that first encounter with the TV set, the computer, or the cell phone like? There are moods, anticipations, and a sense of curiosity that emerge in those first encounters; the uses of media soon become routinized and domesticated.

In her book *When Old Technologies Were New*, Carolyn Marvin (1988) analyzes such processes. She looks back into the nineteenth century, but because media technology has changed so rapidly over the last decades, you don't have to go that far back to find very different situations that can be contrasted with each other. Look at any overview of media literature and you will find materials that have already become cultural history (although the problems addressed may still be the same). You could, for example, use Roger Silverstone and Eric Hirsch's book *Consuming Technologies* (1992), on media use in British homes. Another source is a later ethnography of the everyday, *Busier than Ever!* (Darrah et al. 2007), about stressed Californian families that were using now defunct devices like PDA (personal digital assistants) or pagers. Reading the latter, you will be reminded of a good rule in doing contemporary media ethnography: try writing in the past sense, because it rapidly becomes history.

One good example of a life-history approach is found in Daniel Miller's study of Londoners and their home possessions, *The Comfort of Things* (2008). He entered many homes that were bursting with objects, gadgets, and domestic technologies, but there were also exceptions. Compare his presentations of the lives of Marjorie and Malcolm. Marjorie was in her sixties and lived on her own, but her home was full of mementos, keepsakes, and media stuff relating to relatives and friends.

> *Marjorie's house is where everything is kept, pretty much by everybody. There may be photos in every nook and cranny in her living-room, but they are nothing compared to the three suitcases of photos that she keeps upstairs. . . . But it's not just the photographs; it's the clothes, the keepsakes, the prizes, the toys, the souvenirs from holiday, the paraphernalia of fads.* (Miller 2008: 60)

Miller noted that this type of storage was not a question of hoarding or not wanting to dispose of possessions. Marjorie constantly refashioned herself and her home; media stuff was constantly circulating back and forth between the living room and the boxes in the attic. New collages of photographs and old newspaper clippings were created on the walls; she watched old videos and rearranged knickknacks. In these cycles of replacement and refurbishment, things were always on the move. In the seemingly cluttered disorder, there was a flow of new combinations and associations, producing anecdotes and story links to people.

For Malcolm, who lived down the street, Marjorie's overflowing home would be a provocation. He was in his thirties and also lived alone, often changing lodgings. Growing up with a father who was a collector and antique dealer, he had developed a strong dislike of material possessions. He was constantly ridding himself of things that others would have saved. Books were given away as soon as they were read and clothes discarded.

For Malcolm, the digital era had opened up new possibilities for keeping things and memories while dispensing with them as objects. He used his laptop as an archive and a storage space and devoted many hours to saving and editing photographs, texts, music, and messages. His network, as well as all his personal materials, were sorted, contextualized, and filed in intricate systems. His material surroundings were minimalistic, whereas his laptop was bursting with stuff, yet life was kept in perfect order.

By finding a Marjorie/Malcolm contrast in your interviews, the differences in media use become clearer. These two individuals represent two vastly different ways of handling media stuff; they belong to an analog versus a digital era. The concepts "digital immigrants" and "digital natives" are often used in slightly overdramatized ways, but they can be useful in studying different media generations (Prensky 2001). Marjorie belongs to a generation who grew up in the analog world of the 1950s and 1960s with portable gramophones, tape recorders, Polaroid cameras, and battery radios. She began her office career with typewriters, carbon copies, and index-card boxes, only being exposed later to the new digital technologies.

How can this reschooling from analog to digital media be studied? Searching for historical comparisons, I found two studies of German university students, one from the early 1990s and one from 2011. In the first one, we meet humanities students and teachers who recently have been confronted with the cell phone, the laptop, and the web. Their attitude is slightly suspicious and detached. Is this not just trendy stuff, a temporary fashion? And the web, isn't that simply too commercial? One can almost detect a note of pride when they talk about the minimal and amateurish home page of their university department (Warneken et al. 1998).

In the later interview study, from 2011, young digital natives are compared to older media users (Göess 2011). Many of the latter feel like constant beginners, never catching up with the latest thing: when and where should I go digital? Should I join Facebook? Must I update again? They feel that they are always lagging behind when faced with programs crashing, strange error messages, failed reprogramming, or lost files. The digital natives are much more relaxed about dealing with such minor disasters; they have always lived with them. Both generations, however, have to deal with the constant turnover of technologies and gadgets. In 2011, e-mail felt outdated for the young Facebook generation.

Both generations live at the same time in a crazy mix of analog and digital, switching between pencils and keyboards, Googling and library visits, iPad reading and leafing through print materials. There is a challenge in capturing how all the senses are activated in these activities. Remember Marjorie and Malcolm. What's the difference between carrying a heavy box of photos from the attic, leafing through them by hand, and sorting them into stacks—and surfing between photo files, fooling around with Photoshop, and selecting images for Facebook or deleting something with a simple click?

In a study of media use, the trick is to get people to talk concretely and in detail about how they handle these things. Again, contrasts are helpful, such as asking a middle-aged person to compare her teenage bedroom from the 1970s with the rooms of her own children today. In the 1970s, the room might have been an exciting media lab where different identity projects were playfully tried out with the help of favorite music from a cassette recorder, posing in front of the mirror, writing entries in the carefully hidden diary, choosing posters for the wall, doing collages of movie tickets, fashion drawings, and magazine cutouts on the notice board, and having endless conversations with friends over the phone.

In today's teenager's room, the play with identities might be the same, but the technologies and tools are very different. What does this mean? The time perspective doesn't have to be that long, a few years might suffice. It is the contrasting perspective and the chance to follow gradual changes that are important analytically. They make it possible to unearth the learning processes we want to document. What are the similarities and differences in writing a diary and recording your life on Facebook?

One more reason for finding alternative ways of organizing life-history interviews, whether they are about media or other issues, is that life histories often become a stereotypical genre, a certain way of narrating "my life" from the cradle to the present. People have learned how to present a life by "smoothing" it (see Wilk 2005) and turning it into a neat flow. Afterthought streamlines a development, crowding out detours, paths not chosen, or temporary confusions. Handling objects or doing a walk-along interview at the thrift store can disrupt or provoke such smooth and linear narratives.

In collecting life histories, you will discover how much more rewarding it is to pay attention to small details rather than to larger issues. People often find it easier to begin talking about "my life as a consumer" (car owner, TV viewer, homemaker, etc.) than to talk in general terms about "the joys and sorrows of my life," where the echo chamber effect may be stronger. Paradoxically, talking about mundane things often makes it easier to venture into more personal matters, a tendency we discussed in chapter 3, "Making the Familiar Strange."

MEDIA TAKING PLACE

In the life-history interviews on cultural learning processes, one can follow how media use becomes self-evident. For the ethnographer, the task is to map the web of routines in the everyday, and there are different strategies for this.

First of all, it is easy to forget that some media are so well established that they are no longer seen as that. One way of problematizing how they stand out or not in Western homes is to search for studies of contemporary media use in quite different settings. One example can be found in the work of two anthropologists, Ulrika and Erik Trovalla (2015), who studied everyday life in a Nigerian town that has been ravaged by war and shortages. Electricity was sporadic, making it difficult to keep cell phones charged. Traditional media like radio and newspapers were no help when it came to getting instant news about the fighting and unrest. People found that the most reliable way of obtaining news was to walk out into the street and check the traffic. If it was flowing normally, this was a sign that the city was peaceful today; if there were taxis on their way to the city center, this was a reassuring sign. In a similar manner, sparking electricity cables and creaking water pipes also sent out messages about the current situation. The Trovallas call these alternative information sources that people learned to rely on "infra-media." This is a very different mediascape, and it can inspire us to look for media in corners and situations where we don't expect to find them.

Contrasts can, of course, be used within a narrower range. A group of students were given a week to map habits linked to the cell phone. They began by interviewing themselves and each other but soon realized that they needed to get out and do some observations. They opted for comparing two public settings, a McDonald's and a café. They were struck by the fact that people rarely got out their phones while they were sharing a meal together, but in the café there was a constant flow of both people and messages in and out of the groups at the tables, using their phones.

Gradually the students spotted what they chose to call a kind of "cell phone etiquette." When, where, and how was it okay to answer a call, send a text message, or make a call to someone? As they began to interview people about this, many could talk about these informal rules but found it difficult to remember how they had learned them—it was very much a subconscious process.

The same was the case for Facebook use. There were distinctly shared ideas about how you made yourself interesting, by, for example, signing in from places other than the living room. Facebook use also created ongoing reflections about how to present oneself and one's everyday; again there was a silent cultural understanding. What kind of self-presentations were seen as okay, and which ones seemed too pretentious or could be seen as bragging, and how are such balancing acts learned?

The students' metaphor of cell phone etiquette gave the study a push forward. Thinking of it in terms of etiquette led to a focus on learned norms about proper conduct in given situations. In order to test the limits for the sharing of such cultural rules, the students compared people with different cultural backgrounds, of different genders, ages, and ethnicities. By continually switching between autoethnography, observations, interviews, and discussions in the group, the students collected enough material for several papers.

Another approach was developed by a group of Australian media researchers (Church et al. 2010). They were inspired by the cultural studies scholar John Fiske (1990), who once mapped his own daily media use in order to understand what it did both to his self-understanding and to how he organized his everyday life.

Figure 5.2. Since the early radio days of the 1920s, the sofa has remained the perfect media platform, keeping control of the family. Collective viewing, as in this idyllic photo, is long gone, but the sofa is still there, populated by people surfing, streaming, texting, or gaming—each with a device of one's own. (ThinkStock)

The four Australians transformed their own households into research territories. The first step was defamiliarization; they needed to exoticize their all-too-well-known everyday. They did this by writing about themselves in the third person and by charting everyday details as if they were strange and unfamiliar. All of them wrote a diary of a week, where every instance of making a phone call, watching the TV, listening to music, connecting to the Internet, or swiping their credit card was documented.

Next, they made a plan of their homes and plotted in all the different media and plug-ins, how their media use moved between the rooms, and how it took place. Soon the lines became dense between certain places, and visible paths emerged. The home was described as a mediascape and a web of routines. It turned out that even very mobile media such as laptops and smartphones had their favorite locations. It was interesting to note that there was competition for desirable media spots in the home, as well as the making of private media corners.

By combining diary writing, mapping, and photography, some rich material was generated and different households could be compared. Through this painstaking charting of details, a number of larger issues emerged, the everyday tensions between public and private, for example. How was the global media flow domesticated as it was integrated with home activities, and how did people create new patterns of use? And what was it that made certain old media habits so hard to change? Online news around the clock did not prevent some from turning on the radio or TV news at the traditional six o'clock slot.

New theoretical perspectives were brought in to develop the project further. The group searched for concepts and approaches that would make it possible to see different patterns in the mundane media use. In this case, the duality of "smooth and striated spaces"—taken from the French philosophers Gilles Deleuze and Félix Guattari (1987)—was an eye-opener. The group used "smooth space" to analyze the borderless flows of some media. The laptop travels between being used for watching movies in the bedroom to being a cookbook in the kitchen. The cell phone, when it is taken out of the pocket, transforms a situation or a space. The second term—"striated space"—was used as a tool for studying more place- and time-bound media uses, like the TV set in the dining room, where certain orders and hierarchies were upheld.

By categorization into smooth and striated practices, the researchers could observe how media creates different conceptions of time and space. A similar contrast could be explored in Marjorie's analog everyday and Malcolm's digital one. The point is that analytical concepts such as these may reorganize both the data and the research questions. In the next stage, this can be confronted with alternative theoretical views. For the Australian scholars, the search for theoretical inspiration made it possible to understand how seemingly trivial media habits organized basic understanding of space and time, proximity and distance, home and away. And these were themes that also were emotionally charged, not least in family life.

Reading such a study, it is easy to see what other major issues could be chosen to develop—power struggles in the household, for example. Who controls the remote, or who is the media expert? How are priorities of media use negotiated between children and parents, for example, or in a sibling group?

The Australian exploration of homes could also be expanded by the use of the vast amount of statistics available today that map digital media use. When, where, and how do people surf the web or take out their cell phone? Through online statistics we know a lot more about when high school students do their homework (late on Sunday evenings) and when people log in for Internet banking or watch movies or answer work e-mails. The qualitative analysis of home dynamics of time and place can easily be complemented by statistics that help to pin down more general patterns in rhythms and routines.

Finally, one thing that is striking in the two research examples above is the creative use of a group effort in exchanging reflections and materials. The groups created a forum in which individual media experiences could be tested and compared, and an arena where fieldwork and interview results could be discussed.

VIRTUAL INTIMACY

Following media (such as the smartphone) between different locations and mapping media practices in a domestic scene represent two strategies for tackling media use and habits. Another strategy found in many studies deals with communication over distance, for example, in dispersed families. It is often argued that modern media have been crucial in holding such transnational and migrant families together, for example, a Puerto Rican mother working as a domestic maid in New York to support her children back home, migrant workers who spend long periods away from home, international career makers who are constantly on the move, or illegal immigrants trying to reunite with their families.

Concepts such as "time-space compression," "the death of distance," and "virtual intimacy" have been coined to capture how communication media reorganize distance and closeness, for example, in pulling families together. However, concepts like these need to be critically scrutinized. They risk ending up as one more of the "truths" about modern life that we discussed earlier. So instead of only making rather predictable assumptions about the connecting functions of media, it would be a good idea to turn the argument around. What if new media create new forms of not just contact and intimacy but also distance and alienation?

This kind of critical scrutiny is what the German ethnologist Karin Körber (2012) does in a study of communication in transnational families. What is interesting for our purpose here is that she questions how media technologies, emotional ties, and everyday life interact. Her approach can easily be transferred to other social situations, from parents trying to keep in contact with their kids at college to long-term separations.

Körber's study is built on contrasting diverse experiences of immigrants in Germany. She compares relationships and communication patterns of different generations of migrants—from people leaving all or part of their family behind in order to get "guest worker" status in the 1970s and 1980s, to illegal workers in the early 2000s.

Before the digital era, keeping in contact with family members was done mainly through letter writing and (expensive) long-distance calls. Letter writing produced exchanges that could take weeks, while phone calls often had to be organized in complicated ways. From a public phone booth, people would call one of the few people back in the home village that had a phone and ask her or him to fetch someone from the family, and then they would call again. Both letter writing and short phone calls created their own styles and content of communication that later could be supplemented by sending home messages recorded on cassette tapes—also a very special medium of performance.

It can be said that this kind of mediascape had a strongly ritualized nature. Back then, many migrants felt that being apart from their families was not a personal choice but a fate or the necessity for survival, which made feelings of guilt less of an issue. This was just how life had turned out. Whoever emigrated was simply gone, far away.

Moving into the digital era of the present changed the emotional geography of handling distance and proximity. The wealth of new and inexpensive forms of communication opened up new possibilities but also created new problems.

Let us follow Karin Körber's case study of Ingrida. She is thirty-eight years old and from Lithuania but has been living and working in Germany since 1998. Her daughter, Danuta, who is now eighteen, remained back home in Lithuania with the ageing grandparents. As with so many migrants, Ingrida had planned to stay just for a year or two in order to earn enough money to renovate the family home. An illegal immigrant, she took on all kinds of temporary jobs, but her illegal status made it impossible for her daughter to join her in Germany. Like so many others, Ingrida left her home in order to maintain it, but as is so often the case, this turned into a lasting temporary arrangement.

Over the years, Ingrida has built up a complex system of communication and networks, above all to keep up "long distance mothering" and stay in close touch with her elderly parents and her daughter. There are many practical obstacles. Her old parents can write but find letter writing difficult. They are also hard of hearing, which makes phone conversations problematic. Ingrida has to rely on her sister, who lives next door, to act as a go-between and messenger to the parents. Keeping up with her daughter seemed easier at first as she could get school reports through the school's Internet portal and could e-mail with Danuta's teacher.

When she was able to invest in a computer, a webcam and Internet connections, both in Germany and Lithuania, things seemed to get easier: now they could Skype! The elderly parents could not, however, handle the new equipment, which meant that Ingrida's daughter or sister had to set up any communication, taking away some of the spontaneity of Skyping. But the main problem turned out to be an emotional one. When Danuta turned into a teenager, Ingrida was confronted on Skype with the (not untypical) changes her daughter was going through: nail polish, dyed hair, and a lip piercing.

Long-distance mothering became more difficult. Ingrida started lecturing and could observe her daughter's growing irritation; Skype exchanges became more and more emotional and frustrating. They decided to stop doing it and revert instead to the old medium of a daily e-mail exchange.

> *We write. Whenever we talk we end up arguing. Always, almost every time we talk, I give some kind of sermon and she raises her voice a bit when she responds and that's it. Then it just takes off from there. But when we write, I don't hear her tone since it doesn't come through in the writing. And that's better.* (Körber 2012: 20)

As Körber points out, conflicts between parents and teenagers are part of everyday life, but such conflicts can be handled differently in a face-to-face situation. Doors can be slammed, body language conveys sulking, eyes are diverted at the table—there are all kinds of possible exchanges while the conflict slowly ebbs out or is rekindled. Communicating at a distance often calls for curbing emotions and controlling outbursts of anger that may ultimately lead to contact coming to an end. "I just can't take any more quarrels on Skype!"

Ingrida and Danuta slowly came to realize that changing the form of media used in their communication also changed the quality of their communication. The illusion of closeness or virtual intimacy was exposed. The interplay between the choice of communication technology and their hopes of feeling closer created a complicated emotional landscape. It also opens up the question of how some forms of communication are changed by being turned into ritualized events with culturally defined conventions of performance.

A brief look at the history of telephone conversations may illustrate this. During much of its early history, the phone was predominantly something used by the male middle class and meant for serious and businesslike messages. Long-distance talks with family members or kin had to be arranged in advance and tended to be a rather ceremonial exchange of set phrases: "How are you, we are fine. . . ." In order to boost the medium, telephone companies helped to transform it into a more intimate medium, a strategy of feminization, to gain new users. Slowly, the informal telephone chat developed. Early attempts at introducing video phones were failures, partly because the advantage and intimacy of the phone conversation was the focus on sound. A camera by the phone felt like an invasion of privacy and a nuisance. Still today many people prefer to Skype without the video on.

For Ingrida's elderly parents, a Skype session is a prearranged and probably rather solemn occasion, not at all like a family chat around the table. Letter writing, texting, and e-mailing tend to be rather distinct genres, and we continually need to explore the dimensions of "everydayness" and its effect on media exchanges.

Looking at studies of media keeping families together, it is thus striking that media use often becomes ritualized in everyday life. When, where, and how should you be in contact or be available? What's the difference between a ritualized Sunday morning phone call, a handwritten letter, a text message, and a Skype session? Some migrants try to arrange a virtual presence of their family in their new home, like the nurse from the Philippines working in England who carefully chooses the ringtone signals of her work and family cell phones: a businesslike ring for work-related calls versus a warm and welcoming traditional tune for calls from back home. Two different mood-setting soundscapes are created.

When the nurse moved into a new apartment, she organized a webcam walk through the rooms to try to give her children back in the Philippines a kind of virtual feeling of home in their mother's new setting. An absent family can even be made an everyday virtual presence in other ways, as the flight steward did who always rigged up a little domestic altar with some photos, a few keepsakes, and his laptop screen for Skyping in every hotel room he stayed in. Rituals of virtual togetherness were created.

ARE YOU THERE?

The examples of media uses point to several important research possibilities. It is important to find out how new media creates new divisions of labor, not just the death of old media. Faced with a wider range of alternatives, like Ingrida was, people may choose between various media for different tasks and purposes. Does this message require a Facebook post, a text, a phone call, a post-it note, a proper handwritten letter, or a face-to-face meeting? It is interesting to explore how new media can turn others into nostalgia or give them another status. How are novel hierarchies of authenticity and intimacy created? New media carry not only possibilities but also constraints into everyday life.

Another problem addressed in studies of long-distance communication is the problem of increased accessibility (by cheap and fast media communications) creating increased expectations of dense contacts and swift exchanges. Money or a personal view can be sent digitally at any moment, but still you are not actually "there."

There are some lessons here that can be taken from studies of communication between home and work, where the questions of how cultural norms of attention and availability change. Wanda Orlikowski (2012) followed the introduction of Blackberry phones in an American company. They were introduced to facilitate and speed up e-mails and other forms of communication, but there were no formal rules issued about their use. Orlikowski looked at how expectations of availability and answering slowly developed. How fast did you have to return an e-mail—should it also be done after work? And if so, when? People tried to set their own rules, such as "I never answer anything after work or at least not after 10 p.m.," but slowly work communication invaded domestic life and leisure time. Some people even started answering messages in bed, leading frustrated partners to choose vacation spots that had no Blackberry coverage. By following changing practices over months, Orlikowski could study the social dynamics of a workplace culture without there ever being any master plan. Similar patterns can be analyzed in the cell phone cultures of teenagers or families.

It is important to reflect on virtual and physical presence in relationships. In her book *Cold Intimacies*, Eva Illouz (2007) discusses studies of online dating. She points out how wonderfully easy it is to create an appetizing self-image and fall in love with that image of yourself as well as those of others. People are constantly adjusting and polishing their image of themselves in virtual interactions while projecting their own dreams onto the self-presentation of others. Illouz points out that a disembodied technology may make these self-images seem more authentic:

> *In computer culture, embodiment is often represented as an unfortunate barrier to interaction with the pleasures of computing. . . . In cyber-writing the body is often referred to as "the meat," the dead flesh that surrounds the active mind which constitutes the "authentic self."* (Illouz 2007: 75)

Illouz then goes on to compare virtual meetings with the setting of an actual date at the café table, where bodies and bodily emotions often seem to take up too much space: "Sweaty palms, quickening heart, reddening cheeks, shaking hands, clasped fists, tears, stuttering . . ." In a similar manner, we can see how emotions surface in other ways online than they do in face-to-face communication. It is a question not only of the emotional tones of a virtual romance but also of eruptions of hate mail in cyberspace.

We should follow Illouz's direction and reflect on how technology rearticulates corporality and emotions. This has consequences for the ethnographic approaches chosen. The exciting Internet world has opened up possibilities for everyday research in many new ways. Netnographies based upon Facebook exchanges, home pages, blogs, and so on have proliferated. There is easy access to material, but there are also, of course, some problems of understanding what you are not getting. Many of the best studies of life online combine surfing the Net with interviews and observations.

FOLLOW THE OBJECTS

"People shape their tools of communication that then shape them" writes the media researcher Johan Fornäs (2013: 12), and it is this dialectic that has been the recurrent theme of this chapter: not just media revolutionizing everyday life but everyday life remodeling media. Analyzing this dialectic, the focus has been on learning processes with the help of life-history perspectives and a kind of media archaeology, following objects and practices over time.

To research such learning processes, the term "media literacy" (Hoechsmann and Poyntz 2012) is sometimes used. However, this concept tends to emphasize technological skills more than it does the everyday integration of media practices. Learning to handle media is as much about fitting them into the taskscapes at home. It is about finding times and places for using them, learning to combine them with other activities in ways that make, for example, radio listening into a background noise, TV watching a part of doing the ironing, or going for a walk while checking text messages. Well-established forms of multitasking slowly blend into one activity and are no longer seen as a combination of tasks.

One research question here is about what media activities are well suited for multitasking. Another is about the cultural norms defining what is seen as acceptable behavior. Is it acceptable to text during a meal or at a seminar, or to pick up the phone in the middle of a conversation? There are moral rules here, which change between different settings and different generations of media users.

In order to get at what are often unconscious learning processes, this chapter has advocated the use of contrasting techniques and historical perspectives. You could also try some ethnographic experiments, such as visiting burial grounds for dead or dying media, living offline for a day, writing a media diary, or mapping media flows and practices at home. All of these methodological practices are useful in their own right, but they are also a way of getting better results when interviewing and observing, avoiding some of the pitfalls of life-history narratives.

Running through the discussion has been the idea of following the objects, not only the people. They are coactors. Media studies often tend to underplay this mundane materiality; it gets lost in the flow of texts, sounds, and images. Media use always occurs in a place. What does the bus ride do to the cell phone or the sofa to the laptop? What is the sensual dimension of hammering on the keyboard, juggling the cell phone, or experiencing the warm or stressful light from the computer screen?

Domestic media have a rare capacity to set feelings and moods in action, from nostalgic memories to frustration when they refuse to obey us. Media stuff constantly produces friction. There is the annoyance of searching for a missing password or a DVD, the endless daily drudgery of moving stuff around, or the computer freezing in the middle of downloading new software.

A fragment of a tune, a passing image, or a few written lines can evoke strong memories and feelings; old media may operate as time machines. In her earlier-mentioned study of people constantly moving furniture around in their homes, Pauline Garvey (in Miller 2001: 53) discusses how feelings are changed by shifting the sofa or cleaning the kitchen. The movement of material possessions holds a dynamic, interactive role in this emotional process, she observes.

Is this also true for media stuff? Is the reshuffling of old records, computer files, and boxes of photographs or videos a way of reshuffling life, remaking both the past and the present? Such sensual dimensions in the interaction between people and objects are often hard to capture and call for using the wide range of research tools listed above. As always, it is a good idea to explore one's own experiences of such processes.

Although media has supplied the case material for this chapter, the analytical perspectives discussed can be applied to many other sites and materials where the aim is to make tacit knowledge talk. Think of the wide field of consumption studies or our earlier examples of homemaking and meal sharing. Just ask the two basic (and difficult) questions: what are people actually learning in everyday life, often without their knowing, and how is this learning process possible without handbooks or formal instructions?

6

CATCHING A MOOD

The antihero in Kingsley Amis's novel *Lucky Jim* is a hopelessly disorganized university teacher, but he has one wonderful talent. Entering a new situation or gathering he can swiftly judge the local atmosphere. He calls himself a walking boredom detector: "I am a finely tuned instrument," he adds, and claims that he could be sent ahead into lecture halls, Rotarian meetings, cocktail parties, and nightclubs and quickly come back with the boredom coefficient. "Like a canary down the mine; same idea" (Amis 1953: 215).

Trying to capture everyday moods—from the atmosphere of a seminar room or a party, to the moods inside a commuter train—one can be envious of Jim's ethnographic talents. This chapter moves into the arenas of public life. In recent years, there has been a rising interest in the ethnography of the senses and in attempts to describe an elusive mood or a passing feeling. Trying to capture the sensual dimensions of everyday life means to explore how hearing, seeing, touching, tasting, and smelling work together to define a situation or influence social relations. Ignoring such dimensions of embodied culture makes the ethnography thin.

In the following, we will discuss different strategies for doing ethnography of the senses and putting words to what is often hard to verbalize or even become aware of (a theme that is continued in chapter 7, "Crafting Wood and Words"). The example chosen here —"catching a mood"—is about the making or unmaking of atmospheres in a given place or social situation. The two main themes of the chapter concern what kinds of methods can be used to study a mood and how it often becomes necessary to complement fieldwork with other kinds of materials.

The first advice a student receives when embarking on an ethnographic study is to go to the library, surf the Internet, and look for literature and materials needed to prepare for the fieldwork. The problem is, of course, that at the outset one doesn't really know what to look for. What is interesting? Or important? Beginning a study of a fleeting and elusive phenomenon such as atmosphere, I (in this chapter, Orvar Löfgren) found myself constantly moving between field materials and hunting for inspiration elsewhere. The result is an analytical dialogue that moves back and forth in search of new ideas and inspiration.

LOCATING THE SETTING

First of all, I had to choose an ethnographic arena. Why not study the changing atmospheres of an urban railway station populated by commuters, tourists, and others? Here it would be possible to follow the interaction between bodies, the senses, objects, and movements. The swift changes in tempos, rhythms, and modes in a busy transit space make it possible to observe the interplay between people on the move and the material infrastructure, from platforms to suitcases, as well as how all the senses work together to produce shared moods.

The first step was to observe travelers in the Central Station of Copenhagen, a hub for city commuters coming not only from Denmark but also from Sweden, with the latter taking the train across the border over the newly built bridge that now connects the two countries. I entered the station with camera and notebook, ready to take in all the social life. My first ethnographic attempts did not work. I returned with trivial field notes or sometimes just blank pages and photos that I kept staring at. I felt slightly silly. What other kinds of tools were needed to record and verbalize this elusive world? Any ethnographic project faces the problem of getting stuck at times, of not knowing where and how to look.

Besides traditional sources such as academic writings, I found inspiration in fiction. Many authors are good at putting words to moods and describing small acts and affects in ways that can make an ethnographer envious. There are also the special insights offered by artists who experiment with different ways of problematizing or provoking public arenas like the railway station, from installations to flash-mob performances. Much of this material I found on YouTube, which turned out be a real treasure chest, featuring loads of tourists' videos of railway stations as well as old films and newsreel clips. There are also other rich sources available online, from blogs to the strange home pages of railway enthusiasts. As we pointed out earlier, comparative and contrasting materials can be found almost anywhere.

My first strategy was to distance myself, using a historical perspective, from all that seems to be self-evident in contemporary station life. It is not a question of searching for the origins of public routines and traditions but of going back to a situation when new behavior emerges and people are still wondering how to handle a novel situation; how to move one's body on a bus, for example, or organize a visit to the supermarket. In my case this meant going back to the time when railway travel and station life was born and their routines were slowly taking shape. Merely leafing through a book on the first generation of railway travelers helped me to see how people learned step-by-step to do unfamiliar things like waiting in line, interacting with a sea of strangers, read timetables, or create some privacy in a very public place. Armed with some of these insights of "learning to be a railway traveler," I could return to the field.

ANALYTICAL APPROACHES

The next step was to have a look at the concept of atmosphere itself, and for this, I consulted the online *Oxford Dictionary*. Here I learned that *atmosphere* is a term that has drifted from physics into being a description of emotional moods or situations: from the original meaning of a sphere of gas surrounding a body such as a planet, to a prevailing psychological climate—like the "atmosphere of the court," as the dictionary puts it. Thus it became linked to the concept of mood, defined not only as a personal state of mind but also "applied to a crowd of people or other collective body." It can also be about "the pervading atmosphere or tone of a particular place, event, or period."

It is interesting to note that the original physics of measuring and describing atmospheres traveled over into the study of emotional atmospheres, which themselves are still described like a cultural meteorology: pressure (low/high), weight (heavy/light), temperature (cold/warm), humidity (torrid/steaming). If you ask people to describe an atmosphere, you get answers like "light-hearted," "powerful," "stressful," and "peaceful." They might talk of being overwhelmed, touched, taken in, or moved by a certain mood. Atmospheres can be described as energy reducing, as in inertia, boredom, or anxiety, while others are described as producing positive energy, using terms like euphoric, vitalizing, or just "good vibes." Consider the example of such a phrase as "the energy that rises from the pavements of Manhattan."

Using the concept of atmosphere turned out to be productive in several ways. First, it makes one think about how such moods are produced, sustained, or changed. Second, it opens up the questions of how people come to share an atmosphere or are taken in by it and how it may dissolve boundaries not only between people but also between the body and the material surroundings. Third, it is a concept that focuses on the totality of an emotional mood, on how many different sensual elements are combined: light, color, space, smell, sound, and touch, or movements like rhythm and pace.

Turning to the theoretical literature, I encountered the writings of Gernot Böhme (2006), a German philosopher and architectural theorist who has spent years writing books about the atmospheres in built environments and in both private and public spaces. He has studied the sensualities and aesthetics of everything from colors and textures to what he calls the "ecstasies of things." His approach is shaped by an architectural tradition and the search for ways to understand how good feelings can be created in buildings. But he doesn't really tackle how to do ethnography of these themes. I had to look elsewhere.

"Is there anyone who has not, at least once, walked into a room and 'felt the atmosphere'?" asks Teresa Brennan (2004: 1) in the introduction to her book *The Transmission of Affect*. She is interested in how people are emotionally affected by others. Her focus is on how an atmosphere is felt on and in the body, a communication that dissolves the boundaries between the individual and the environment. Teresa Brennan explores the different roles of the senses. She draws on neurological research on the transmission of hormones (running through the blood) and airborne molecules of pheromones (registered on the skin).

There is no need to go further into such neurological discussions here; what is important is that the nervous system registers and reacts to the emotional climate of another person, a group, or an environment. Again, there is the tricky question of how people become part of such a climate. Think, for example, of a nervous atmosphere that is communicated by body signals and even more by tingling sensations—"nervousness is in the air." Brennan challenged me to begin looking for contagious atmospheres.

Looking for a more detailed ethnographic approach, I turned to a study of Jamaican dance halls, "The Vibrations of Affect and Their Propagation on a Night Out on Kingston's Dancehall Scene" (Henriques 2010). Like Brennan, Henriques is interested in the transmission of affect, but his focus is on "the feeling the vibes" and on trying to find ways of measuring the intensity of atmospheres.

Reading these texts, I was struck by how feelings and moods are often described through metaphors. This makes it a good idea to think about how such metaphors may influence our own way of framing or understanding an event. What happens to the analysis when we think of atmosphere in terms of "vibes" or a special "climate," or of a feeling as a "gut reaction"?

TOURING THE SENSES

I returned to the train station with these three authors and their very different approaches in mind. Teresa Brennan argues that shared atmospheres are created not so much by visual impressions as by the ear, the nose, and the skin, three subtle forms of communication. Sound, smell, and touch work more directly than sight, which is a sense that separates and selects more than do other senses, as she points out.

The visual had, of course, been my ethnographic starting point. I went to the station with the camera, looking, staring, glancing—my eyes perhaps too wide open. The other sensual impressions were just background disturbances. Now I couldn't help thinking about the kind of lighthearted advice we give students on how to do sensual ethnography: "Don't fall into the trap of giving the visual any primacy: close your eyes, use a recorder for sounds, and try to 'feel' the atmosphere." Easier said than done, but I returned to the Copenhagen Central Station once again, wanting to explore other sensual inputs.

I went back on an August Sunday in the middle of the holiday season and started to record the soundscape with my cell phone. The first thing that struck me was the diffuseness of the background noise; it was as if all kinds of sounds were blended into a constant murmur. I tried to identify the various ingredients of that mixture: voices, steps, luggage being dragged along, and the faint humming of the escalators. Some sounds stood out from this constant murmur: the clickety-clack of the wheels of bags and suitcases being hauled along the stone floor, bits and pieces of conversations drifting past, the sudden "ding-a-dong" signaling the loudspeaker announcements with their messages booming out into the air, and a returning, rather stressful and angry flow of signals from some kind of invisible machine: "beep-beep-beep."

If sound was difficult to handle, smell was even worse. On the Internet, I found a cry for help. "How does a station smell?" someone asked, trying to write an essay. The first answer she received was: "Do stations smell? I'll have to find out next time."

Terms such as "smellscapes" have been coined to attempt to capture olfactory scenes. But smell is one of the least-recorded and least-discussed senses. In this field, the terminology often seems even vaguer or less developed than it does for sound. Some special fields are much elaborated, as in the poetics of perfume and wine tasting, but on the whole, it is a fairly limited vocabulary, often focusing on the unpleasant smells—acid, musty, stale—and drifting over into the universe of taste. In this sensory realm, the polarity between pleasant and unpleasant seems more marked than for many other senses. Even words such as "odor," "aroma," "smelly," and "bouquet" are loaded with positive and negative connotations. And, again, the metaphorical landscape is rich, as in the "sweet smell of success" or being "stinking rich."

I went back to the station ready to explore smells, lacking an olfactory recorder but relying on paper and pen. Does Copenhagen Central Station smell? My first impression was no. It seemed hard to describe the smells of the station, although I slowly began to identify some. Maybe I am one of those many people who haven't developed strong olfactory skills, unlike a female colleague. When this colleague accompanies me, I get much more input. Walking into a café for lunch, she stops at the entrance and tells me that the

Figure 6.1. Surviving in transit spaces like this London underground station calls for multitasking skills: coordinating your body movements with the crowd, looking for flashing departure signs while trying to catch strange loudspeaker noises. (ThinkStock)

place just doesn't smell good enough to eat there. When I ask her what it smells like, she takes another whiff and answers: "It feels stale, the air is dense, a strange mix of not very appetizing food flavors, sweating customers, stressed staff. Let's go somewhere else; I don't feel comfortable here."

Again, my olfactory searches in the station made me unfocused. It was time to visit the Net again. Surfing among ethnographies of smell, I found a useful paper, a study of smoking in urban spaces in Singapore (Tan 2012). The author's assumption is that over the last years smoke has become a highly contested element in public spaces. He follows smokers around, locates their spaces and behaviors as well as the reactions of nonsmokers. In the heydays of smoking in public it was hardly noticed, it was everywhere. Now it evokes angry reactions or moral judgments. It has started to smell in new intolerable ways, and smokers are increasingly marginalized. As Qian Hui Tan points out, the olfactory politics around this habit reveal much about segregation and stratification in public spaces, but it is also an example of what kinds of sharing are seen as undesirable, or, in this context, unhealthy.

As an ex-smoker, I can register not only my own diminishing tolerance but also my heightened olfactory awareness—I can now spot the merest whiff of it. Before I returned to the station to explore the changing landscape of cigarette use, I searched for old photos and film clips of earlier station life. It didn't take long to see that people used to smoke constantly and everywhere in the station. Gradually, this was restricted to certain areas, from special compartments in trains to certain outdoor spaces like the platforms.

Today, I find the smokers driven out of the station altogether. At the main entrance, I have to pass through a dense wall of smoke. This is where they have to gather, creating temporary communities. I saw people making detours around them in order not to be contaminated by the smell. Smoking that was once so glamorous, full of sex appeal and sophistication, now attracted irritated and slightly condemning glances. The station entrance had, in a sense, been turned into a morally contaminated area populated by losers.

Focusing on smoke was a good way to get an entrance into smellscapes. On the Net, I found other discussions of station smells. A German company worked hard to produce a perfume that evoked the special burnt smell of trains as they braked on entering the station. This, they felt, was a scent people could identify.

At the Copenhagen station, I kept wondering about what kinds of smells are present when we describe something as odorless. Does boredom, stress, or irritation have an aroma? There is a rich field waiting to be explored here; just start asking and sniffing around. On a platform, I heard a woman telling her friend, "I never travel second class; I just can't stand that smell of orange peels."

After soundscapes and smellscapes, it was time to explore the registers of the haptic (any form of nonverbal communication involving touch). It has been argued that the skin is not only our largest sensory organ but that it is also extremely important in the ways we register and are influenced by local atmospheres. The haptic dimension is, of course, present in the ways people handle the material world of the station. To be able to do ethnography of this sensual register, it is good to pay attention to details, for example, by spending an hour observing only how people handle handbags or cell phones. What kinds of small movements can be registered here? I spent some time watching five people on a bench and their continuous interaction with their travel stuff—rummaging through their wallets, rearranging baggage, fidgeting with or clutching stuff—and trying to make some notes.

When you are in a state of anxious travel fever, holding on to objects becomes important. There can be comfort in clenching a handbag, toying with the ticket, feeling the warmth of a cup of coffee, or taking refuge in your own temporary home on a bench defended by your luggage.

Returning to Gernot Böhme's work, it was possible to explore how the materiality of the station building affects the senses. The gigantic arrival hall makes people smaller. The flow of light from the glass roof, the hard marble floor, and the lack of hideouts and sheltered corners make the scene very public.

It was also possible to observe how people handled physical contact with others, but it took some time until I could register all the silent body communications, the small gestures and instant affects. I watched averted faces but also quick smiles, irritated elbows, and helping hands. People got pushed, tripped over luggage, and squeezed past others. They were monitoring an acceptable distance while standing in line or sitting down close to others.

I felt like getting out a mental measuring rod and comparing how close people sit to each other on a shared bench. Tools for such studies can be borrowed from the field of proxemics, with its comparisons of how different groups define acceptable closeness or distance in public situations (a classic of this kind of study is Hall 1959). I constantly had to monitor my ethnographic gaze; in urban settings, people have learned to not stare but just glance at strangers, but these unwritten rules change in different settings. Think about your own travel experiences and forms of eye contact. When do you feel comfortable or uncomfortable in a sea of strangers?

THE STATION AS A SENSORIUM

Many of these ethnographic attempts raised more questions than they produced results. One problem is that the senses are intensely entangled with each other. Just as scholars have been busy categorizing and labeling emotions, the talk of separating the five senses can be rather unproductive. At the railway station, I was reminded of all the ways smell and sound work together, and of how the hands work with the eyes. When I heard the stressful signals, I immediately conjured up an image of angry red blips from a hidden warning lamp. Listening to my recording from the station at home was also a very one-dimensional experience. Instead of thinking in terms of five separate senses, it will be good to look for concepts that bridge them and might show how they work together or block each other.

It is also a good idea to design small experiments of measurement. If you find it hard to gauge the mental temperature of a place, try determining the actual temperature with the help of a thermometer. How do the climates of the different station areas change? In a similar manner, try a cell phone app to assess the decibel strengths of different soundscapes. My point here is that it often works to mix such experiments of physics and informal statistics with the cultural analysis of sensual dimensions that are hard to transform into figures. How does it feel to move between spaces with different temperatures? Does a soundscape of x decibels sound noisier than one of y decibels?

I also returned to the literature in order to get a focus. One of Henriques's concepts is "intensity"—on several levels. What are the intensities of the sensual inputs and their effects: getting a whiff of something or being engulfed by a stench; being surrounded by a din or barely registering a hushed or soft sound. In the same way, there is the question of impact; some sensory inputs catch us unaware and unprepared, and render us defenseless. Over time we can learn to overlook, overhear, or stop noticing a smell.

Another central concept in Henriques's approach is that of "rhythm," a notion that spans many senses and sensations. People fall in and out of sync with moving crowds; there are sudden changes between feelings of stress and bored waiting. Different rhythms clash both in the body and in the station crowds, from individual heartbeats to surging flows.

CHANGING MOODS

I took these concepts of intensity and rhythm back to the station with me and used them for another classic ethnographic approach. I worked with contrasts in order to get elusive traits to surface and find out how moods change over time and in different social situations. First of all, I moved from space to space in the station complex, registering changes in atmospheres and how the senses worked together.

Walking into the crowded ticket office from the vast arrival hall, sounds became much more muted, and here, standing in line, I also felt the body odors of impatience and irritation. The atmosphere was denser here, space more cramped. The lowered ceiling took away the strong echo effect of the main hall. Moving on down to the platform area, body languages changed. Energy was now focused on the rails and the information screens. There was a lot of staring along the tracks as if a late train could be conjured up by staring into the void.

Leaving the station, I took the passage that leads out to the Copenhagen red-light district. Here the atmosphere changed abruptly. Classical music was being played, loud and a bit too fast. I found an online newspaper article head-lined: "Verdi and Wagner Keep the Junkies Away." The journalist stated that "undesirable elements" had a tendency to gather here—that is, the homeless, drunks, and junkies—and the station manager had introduced loud classical music in an attempt to drive the vagrants out of the passage. The place was soon abandoned. A waiting arena was turned into an uncomfortable and un-inviting space just by changing the soundscape. What other techniques may be used to make a space inviting or uninviting?

Apart from this drastic change of scene, I found it hard to register and characterize the different climates of the station area. I needed another con-trast and turned to observing changes in the atmosphere around the clock by returning at different hours and weekdays.

I began late one morning by following a couple of tourists who were hesitantly dragging their baggage around, searching for information. How did I come to define them as tourists, what signs was I looking for? Their body movements gave them away as newcomers. They were scanning the terrain for all kinds of information, moving around slowly, and really looking lost.

All of a sudden, the arrival hall fills up, a late commuter train has arrived and the atmosphere changes drastically. The commuters move swiftly, like a military phalanx plowing its way through the tourist travelers, who try to get out of the way but here and there are surrounded like islands in the fast flow of commuters striding along the floor, their gazes fixed into the distance. Mentally, they may already be at work, and they do not observe the station surroundings at all. There is no hesitation in their bodies—just the same old morning routines. They are the station veterans.

In just a few moments, the stream ebbs out and the station returns to its lethargy. The tourists are in control again, together with the homeless and the others who use the station as their temporary urban refuge or meeting place, surreptitiously checking for the guards or police who patrol round the station.

YouTube offered additional material, with lots of visitors recording their first encounter with the Copenhagen station. There was a film clip, for example, by a young American with a running commentary added; here was the station landscape through the eyes and lens of two enthusiastic tourists: "Wow, look over there. Awesome! And hey, there is even a McDonald's."

My own experiences also gave me some insights into the station rhythms. Moving among the rush-hour crowds that confidently were hurrying through the station complex, I registered in my own body what it is to be out of sync; I felt like a country bumpkin. I have lived too long in a small town where I just visit the metropolis; and I realize that I have lost some of the skills of maneuvering in fast crowds. I can't read the signals, my body movements are indecisive; not part of the flow, I am often about to bump into people. Sometimes, I can read slight irritation in the eyes of the efficient commuters and remember the classic Copenhagen saying about incompetent newcomers: "Did you just arrive on the four o'clock train?" My failure at least gave me some autoethnographic insights into what it feels like to be out of sync among people, as well as a chance to reflect on what skills I lacked.

The morning rush hour gave the station a very special quality. There was a feeling of expectancy in the air—the start of a fresh working day, a kind of positive stress. Later in the day the tempo slowed down, and the soundscape and the mood were different, with the echoes of solitary travelers moving along the hall. As the tired commuters returned later in the day to go home, the station had a different feel. Compare this to the festive mood of the station on a Friday or Saturday evening, when groups of people are arriving and leaving in search of a fun night out. It forced me to think about how we define a mood like "a party feeling" as well as to reflect on how such a mood becomes contagious.

Recording these rhythms and intensities, I felt the need for more inspiration and turned to a classic site, so often depicted in movies: New York's Grand Central Terminal, with its bustling crowds. In a study of space, Tony Hiss (1991: 98) watches the crowds here and reflects about the social skills you need to learn to handle this setting. He observes

the swirling, living motion of five hundred people walking, two and three abreast, from and toward the fourteen entrances and exits of the concourse. Moving silently, as it seemed, within that sound, I noticed again that no one was bumping into anyone else—that every time I thought I myself might be about to bump into people near me, both I and they were already accelerating slightly, or decelerating, or making a little side step, so that nobody ever collided. On top of this, the weightless sensation in my head gave me the feeling that I could look down on all this movement, in addition to looking out at it. I had a sense that the cooperation I was part of kept repeating itself throughout the vast room around me and the vaster city beyond it.

How is this collective choreography made possible, with its coordination of hundreds of different styles of walking and moving? Here is a competence of quick glances, body signals, and swift movements.

Searching on YouTube for scenes at Grand Central Station, I found a flash-mob project, where two hundred actors at a given signal froze their movements in the commuter crowd. The hidden camera records how all of a sudden the flow stops and amazed fellow passengers look around trying to understand what is happening. It is like the whole arrival hall holds its breath for a moment. By provoking and sabotaging the routine, normality all of a sudden becomes visible.

I found many other such flash-mob projects on YouTube as well as a number of sites where hundreds of movies with station scenes were listed (just Google "station-setting movies" and you will discover a gold mine). Versions of station life from movies are often good because they highlight the dramatic potentials of a very mundane commuter arena.

To turn to the literature on body movements, the classic is Erving Goffman's (1967) study of people moving in crowds on urban pavements. In a later comment on this study, Tim Ingold (2011) points out that, although it is an inspiring pioneer attempt to capture urban choreographies, Goffman's study has very few bodies, limbs, and feet in it and too many eyes. To read the ways these two authors present different ethnographic strategies for studying the same scene is quite illuminating and made me reflect on the choices of words and perspectives in my own field notes.

DESCRIBING ATMOSPHERES

In trying to capture the changing flows and moods of the Copenhagen station, I also looked for comparative descriptions made by fiction writers and journalists who have used the station as a scene. In a novel from the 1930s describing the urban mentality of Copenhagen, the author follows his main character in and out of the Central Station, picturing the changing moods. One winter's day, the hero walks into the station at noon and finds it almost deserted, apart from a few bored jobless men hanging about. The writer describes the cold and damp draught from the platforms and continues:

> *The sound of a solitary suitcase at the other end of the hall. One's own steps sound unintentionally energetic against the tiles—the whipping sound of sharp heels—and the air above carries a faint hum like the one coming from a shell. And all of a sudden something comes over you—there is something important you are missing. A*

sudden urge to just jump on a train and get out of this depressing city. (Sønderby 1931: 124)

Much later, writing about her impressions of the Copenhagen station when waiting for the midnight train back to Sweden, the commuter Julia Svensson (2010) portrays the mood of frustration and depression that may take over the station at night. The train is, as always, late. The cafeterias close, and after that there is only the chill of the platforms and the arrival hall:

On platform 5, I found the Swedish commuter who turned into my first real Copenhagen friend. We shared being cold and also feeling frozen out. We had been evicted from McDonald's. We had tired of looking at the model train by the railway café. We were tired of the fact that our time seemed worthless for the Danish State Railways. Most days you don't want to meet new friends, most days you just want to get home.

"Everything is closed"—all the closed shutters and locked doors help to produce a feeling of being left out. The passengers become a group of losers who are marginalized, outside of society. The mood becomes slightly depressive, gone is all the morning energy of early travel. The environment no longer seems welcoming; the station is transformed into a hostile place.

Descriptions like these made me return to Teresa Brennan's discussion of atmospheres as contagious—a silent communication and sharing. I turned to my own commuter experiences. I started taking notes one day when the train was delayed and stopped in the middle of nowhere. At first I found myself relaxing, continuing to read the fascinating book I had brought with me. Slowly, I registered the growing irritation and frustration inside the carriage. The mellow, almost meditative mood was gone. People began to communicate their frustration with sighs and shrugs. Many turned to their mobile phones in their need to have an audience and complained loudly about being stuck on the train "again!" "I hate this train," said a girl near me into her phone.

I noticed how I was influenced by the changing atmosphere. I tried to stick to my book and the earlier feeling of bliss, but no, my body was invaded by the collective mood—at first as a vague anxiety, then as a lump in the stomach. I stared at my watch; the book could not hold my attention any longer.

At last, the train moved. But now, my and the other passengers' feelings of stress had grown, and this became evident when we finally arrived at the Copenhagen station. All of a sudden, things could not move fast enough. I became aware that I was staring angrily at a man who was taking too much time to get his stuff organized. I was not the only one who now had a short fuse as the atmosphere became short tempered; gone was the meditative mood of commuting. The delay lasted maybe fifteen minutes, but I carried it around in my body for the rest of the day.

INTIMATE MOODS

The station experience deals with atmospheres produced on a vast arena in a complex setting. What happens if we take the concept into a quite different context?

At the station there are people with earphones everywhere. People are listening, creating not only their own private bubbles but also their own emotional microclimates. If you want to understand how moods are produced in different settings, music listening is not a bad place to explore.

Sometimes when I listen to songs I see images, like pictures in front of me, and things that happen, and feelings. (Werner 2012: 1)

This is Billie, a fourteen-year-old girl, part of a study on how music and moods come together in everyday life. The gender researcher Ann Werner decided to hang out with teenage girls, girls who had their earphones on wherever they went, listening to music on the commute, at school, or at home in their room. She was interested in how music was used as a mood-setting tool in different ways and situations. For these girls, music was a way to create collective moods or add a personal note to a public setting, like walking down the school corridor with the earphones dangling from their shoulders and their music seeping out.

Werner asked the young girls how they themselves classified and chose music not in terms of trends and styles but in relation to their moods. Doing a "folk taxonomy" on people's ways of classifying and ordering their everyday activities can be a fruitful part of an ethnographic study.

Three themes, "cheerful music," "awful music," and "sad music," emerged as the main categories for these girls. Werner called them emotional clusters, because they were complex mixes and combinations of feelings and moods. "Cheerful music" was very much linked to energizing movements, tapping your feet, moving your hips, or dancing in front of the mirror; there might be a mix of smiling, longing, dancing, and a certain amount of happy craziness. "Sad music" also had many dimensions, not only as sadness connected to lost love or other troublesome issues but also as a kind of bittersweet melancholy and nostalgia in a mix that could change from unpleasant to enjoyable. "Sad music" was often peaceful and slow, which worked fine when one was tired or doing homework.

The next step in the study concerned the creation of space. Werner found that the headphones were used as a device to shut oneself off from a surrounding, for example, the bustle of the station. They were also used to avoid contact with people you didn't want to interact with—like the person next to you on the train.

One day, Ann Werner saw one of the girls, Sarah, slumped on a bench in the school corridor with her MP3 player. Sarah said she often used music to create a personal free zone, an escape from the tough school atmosphere. Her body language signaled that she was in a world of her own and should not be disturbed.

A study like this could be developed in many directions. Studying music turns out to be a good way of understanding mood settings and mood changes in both private and collective situations. A further analysis could combine other sensory tools: lighting, food, visual images, and so on. Werner's study opens up possibilities to watch actors who, by being the life and soul of the party to being the killjoys, actively (or unconsciously) change atmospheres in a public setting—what kinds of powerful silent signals are they sending out?

CHANGING TRACKS

Comparing my own station ethnography with Ann Werner's study, several methodological themes stand out. One is to keep mixing and combining approaches. In order to get on with my fieldwork, I had to constantly search for inspiration elsewhere: in novels, flash-mob performances, or railway movies. The cell phone became a multipurpose tool, from a recording device to a means of accessing YouTube.

First, I realized that I had to develop new skills when dealing with visual stuff. By looking at video clips from my station visits over and over again, I discovered new details. Looking at a film clip, you may see nothing at first, but by freezing, forwarding, rewinding, and scrutinizing (a certain person in the filmscape, for example), eventually you might see something surprising. (To take the visual analysis further, there are a number of good handbooks; see, for example, Pink 2007.) So much ethnographic work is based on this kind of movement back and forth between different approaches and materials. Such a methodological technique creates dynamics that are hard to pin down and even remember when the study is finished.

Second, I learned to stop "just looking" and instead focus on minor details or certain behaviors, experimenting with different kinds of ethnographic material, as well as with autoethnographic observations.

Third, I was triggered by a concept developed by the cultural geographer Doreen Massey (2005). She talks about how places are created by the "thrown-togetherness" of people, matter, tasks, and affects, making them unpredictable arenas. The station may seem like a very stable bricks-and-mortar monument, but it is really built by all the comings and goings, as well as by the very diverse tasks, motives, and mental luggage that are dragged into it. It is a messiness created by the constant interweaving of the ebbs and flows of people, heavy luggage, malfunctioning ticket machines, loud music, and all kinds of sensory inputs. The ethnographic task is to explore how this mess works together— uniting or separating events, people, and objects.

The mixing of materials and approaches is also found in Ann Werner's study. The major difference is that she followed a group of actors around closely and also interviewed them, even in group discussions. The girls liked to talk about what music did to them and how it affected their moods. As they all used digital forms of communication—chatting about music, sharing tunes, making lists of favorites—netnography was important. It would have been tempting to just use this kind of easily accessible material. However, Ann Werner realized that this would have led her to miss important dimensions that could only be gotten from actual fieldwork observations—from body language and rapidly passing affects, to uses of space and movement. In the building of mood, both the body and the environment are important actors. Again, the teenage rooms and the school corridors are examples of Massey's "throwntogetherness."

Figure 6.2.   What's the mood? "Leave me alone," "just bored waiting," or "happy daydreaming" . . .? Creating a microclimate with headphones is easy. (Adina Ehn)

Finally, contrasting was an important part of Werner's fieldwork and in the choice of informants. She compared two different schools, making sure that the girls had different social and ethnic backgrounds. Her overarching question was gendering in everyday life. Music, mood, and emotions brought a number of existential questions up to the surface. What kinds of female identities are produced among the young girls? Reading this study, one realizes how differently boys of the same age handle music and moods, but there are other contrasting potentials. At a later stage, Ann Werner did a comparative study with a colleague who studied Australian girls (Cahir and Werner 2013). What turned out to be global similarities and local differences? To find an international collaborator can be quite a project in itself, but by searching for studies with similar themes as your own, you might find contrastive materials.

This made me think about what would have happened if I had chosen Werner's approach and stuck with a group of commuters, sharing their experiences and interviewing them. I found two other studies that illustrated this approach. Louise Nielsen (2012) followed a group of veteran long-distance commuters into Copenhagen, traveling with them and interviewing them again and again. Her approach made it possible to see how travel skills develop and strangers turn into fellow commuters. Laura Straw (2008) carried out similar fieldwork in England and looked at railway travel as "an art and a craft"—not a bad concept. Both of them also discuss how moods could change during a journey and even between different train carriages.

SENSING THE WORLD

Atmosphere is an important topic in several ways. First of all, it highlights how people may react to certain situations without really understanding the ways they are being drawn into a certain mood. Second, it opens up questions about the relations between individual and collective feelings. How are moods and feelings transmitted—at a party, in a seminar room, or at a political rally, for example? They are also selective in that they might make some people feel welcome and others unwelcome. Who belongs at the railway station? For me, the station ethnography was an example of small details opening up larger issues. I became interested in the ongoing discussion of urban commons in modern cities. How are people included or marginalized in public spaces?

There are a number of other places and situations suited for ethnography of moods, from waiting rooms to Saturday night parties. Step-by-step, it is possible to grasp the elusive processes that make or unmake a mood and that create shared or different experiences among those present. Suddenly you see what is actually happening; for example, when registering a change of temper or understanding silent forms of communications. By activating all the senses and testing analytical tools like rhythm, intensity, and props, a new analytical dimension in the study of everyday life emerges.

To describe moods calls for a combination of a number of analytical and ethnographic tools that make it possible to turn into words what otherwise disappears without a trace. Things are registered in a glimpse, a passing hunch, or a fleeting image.

By training yourself to write field notes from a boring commute or a seminar room, the analytical attention is sharpened. By activating all the senses, it becomes possible to picture moods and mood changes. It is not only a question of enriching ethnography; it is also a question of not shutting out important parts of everyday life from the analysis. Emotions energize social situations. A high (or extremely low) energy level may alert the researcher that something important is going on here that can redefine a situation. An atmosphere seeps into both the mind and the perception of the surrounding: turning a prospect rosy or coloring a setting a melancholy grey.

7

CRAFTING WOOD AND WORDS

Writing this chapter has been an extraordinary experience. Never before have I (in this chapter, Billy Ehn) thought so much about writing as physical work, as a kind of handicraft. What I mean by this will soon be explained. Let me just tell you initially that there is much that cultural researchers can learn from doing practical things with their hands—like carpentry, for example—and then trying to describe and analyze it in detail. As will be clear, crafting wood and crafting words are not at all dissimilar activities.

ETHNOGRAPHIC WRITING

Doing ethnography and cultural analysis is mainly about writing—from scribbling down the first ideas and making field notes to composing a paper or a book. You have to master a special kind of writing, which, among other things, means combining personal storytelling with a strict analytical language. You also have to obey certain supportive academic rules for writing at the same time as you search for your own way of expressing thoughts and interpretations. This is a demanding task, to say the least.

Since the publication of *Writing Culture: The Poetics and Politics of Ethnography*, edited by James Clifford and George Marcus (1986), there has been an ongoing debate about various forms of ethnographic writing. Many researchers from different disciplines have argued for more literary and experimental styles of writing "messy texts" (Denzin 1997), such as autoethnographies, ethnodramas, short stories, memoirs, personal histories, and even poetry (see, for example, Ellis 2004 and Goodall 2000).

On the other hand, these "poetic" texts have been criticized for being subjective, narcissistic, too personal, or just plain bad writing. They have not always been considered as acceptable scholarship when it comes to grading papers, judging publications, and obtaining grants. So even if you can claim that most scientific writing is, in a way, storytelling, you have to be clever when you choose your style, perspective, and level of analytical abstraction, balancing carefully between experimental ethnography and established demands, especially when you want to be published in a peer-reviewed book or journal. When writing field notes or a diary, the conventions are much looser.

MAKING THINGS WITH WORDS

In the second chapter of this book, about the five steps of the research process, we said that writing is a creative activity that you don't have total control over: it is guided by emotions and fantasies in unexpected ways; nevertheless, at the same time, you are expected to follow methodological rules.

This theme will now be developed through the example of a concrete case. The aim is to show how you can practice ethnographic writing and learn more about language as both a subjective and an objectifying medium. To accomplish this, I try different ways of describing and interpreting a personal experience.

My case is rather down-to-earth. I will discuss writing about a seemingly simple physical everyday activity: a summer weekend carpentry project in which I produced duckboards for my shower floor. By switching between making things out of wood and out of words, I want to get a better understanding of writing as both an intellectual and a physical activity—a kind of handicraft.

Switching between writing and carpentry has made me more observant of what is going on, both when I write on the laptop and when I work with the carpenter's tools. On a closer look, crafting wood and crafting words have some interesting similarities. You transform a chosen material into something else by procedures that you have to learn and master. Exploring everyday life as an ethnographer means confronting it in ways that often are not quite conscious and then translating it into something more substantial in the form of descriptions, stories, and analyses.

The point here is that writing ethnography and doing cultural analysis are practical matters, just as carpentry is. They are not only intellectual labor but are also about accomplishing several hands-on tasks with your body and your senses, working with other people and with material objects. Doing cultural analysis and writing also involves your emotions. Writing is a skill learned by doing, and it includes both experiments and rewritings. Learning to handle failures is an important part of that process, a subject I will return to later.

When you are writing and thinking—when producing a student essay, for example—you are making something with words. This means that you are consciously using special tools, skills, and bodily movements in order to fulfill your intellectual aims and plans. It also means that you are doing several things without consciously thinking about them—a theme that permeates this book—because you have learned them so well that they are performed automatically. Then the words seem to start meaning something to you. A lot of mixed feelings will either help or might disturb you in the research process, like the joys of when writing flows, the tedium of cleaning up a text, and the frustration of writer's block. Writing can indeed be both a manic and depressive activity.

By reflecting on these practical, mental, and emotional aspects of research, you will be better prepared to manage the difficulties in doing ethnography and cultural analysis. These include the times when you get stuck in your writing, when you run out of ideas, when you are too self-critically dissatisfied with your text, or when, on the contrary, you think uncritically and prematurely that you have finished a masterpiece.

AUTOETHNOGRAPHIC WRITING

Switching between writing and physical work can be looked upon as a movement between two separate realities, where body and mind are used in different ways. But it can also be experienced as a more unified event. I shall discuss this latter experience using an autoethnographic method, similar to the one used in the chapter on sharing meals, reflecting on my own work, thoughts, and feelings.

Over recent years I have become an enthusiastic do-it-yourself (DIY) person with a hammer, saw, screwdriver, and other tools. But the following autoethnography could just as well be about other practical tasks like knitting, cleaning, sailing, or playing football. How do you describe such physical activities? This is the first problem I will deal with.

The second problem concerns what it means to observe and write about yourself doing practical things and which methodological tools you use in such a case. Autoethnography is a method frequently employed today (see, for example, Chang 2008). In most cultural and social investigations, the researchers certainly use themselves as a kind of research tool to describe and understand various phenomena but usually without making it the main method or even without reflecting on it at all. The autoethnographer's experiences may therefore enhance the understanding of the subjective and reflexive aspects of research. By doing this you learn more about how the interpretations of other people's behavior are influenced by the researcher's personal background and education, among other things.

The practice of ethnography may be described as a continuous oscillation between observing, listening, thinking, interpreting, writing, reading, sensing, discovering, and making new observations. In this heavy intellectual and sensory traffic, the researcher confronts a mix of frustration, joy, and new energy. This means you have to prepare yourself for emotional turns and have the courage to finish the fieldwork, continue to write, and finally present a text for critical readers. My experience is that autoethnography is a good way to crisscross between feelings and reflections. It makes you a more sensitive fieldworker.

Theoretically, autoethnography is related to what has been called "the more-than-representational perspective" (Vannini 2012, 2015) in research into everyday actions, emotions, and experiences. Using this perspective the ethnographer tries to verbalize her or his own practices and sensations, and to analyze how these interact with the social and material surroundings. This means that culture is studied in the intersection between the private and the public, between the silent doing and the more-communicative interaction. Concerning my own case as an amateur carpenter, I am embedded in both a seemingly lonely work at home and the mass movement of DIYers that is manifested in the media and the market.

The paradox is that I am doing ethnographic research with some of the scientific tools that we described earlier in this book, while, almost at the same time, I am also working with the carpenter's tools. The simultaneous crafting of wood and words arouses some crucial questions about how to study practical knowledge and how to become more conscious about what is going on when you are writing ethnography.

The use of autoethnography and experiments of self-narrative should contribute to the improvement of both fieldwork and writing. In fact, all ethnography may be seen as a kind of DIY project. You are using yourself, your body, your mind, and your personality, not just scientific methods, to generate knowledge. In this process you are learning by doing through trial and error, as when you learn how to fix things at home. All the time you have to ask if your method of producing materials and ideas is working. Are the field notes good enough for your purposes? Is the analysis well thought out? Are the interpretations interesting?

You can never be sure of how to accomplish these undertakings in the right way since, in spite of all the handbooks, there are in fact very few solid rules to guide cultural research in real life. Therefore you must do a lot of experimenting along the way. Autoethnography is a helpful technique to learn more about the complexity of doing fieldwork and writing about it. You will get to know more about how research material is produced in situ. Otherwise it is easy to forget all the mess before the text is finished. You may also wish to conceal the untidiness in order to present a more systematic picture of the research process. Then, even the professional ethnographers feel perhaps like DIYers when they are in the field as well as when they are writing about it, trying to understand what is going on.

DESCRIBING NONVERBAL EXPERIENCE

Until the duckboards project, I had not thought much about my DIY activities, at least not from a reflexive and an analytical point of view. Being at once both leisure and work, they have been fun to do, although often rather demanding. I experience them as a relaxation from sedentary academic duties, as an expansion of my practical competence, and as a strengthening of my masculine identity in a stereotypical way. But when you look at it more closely, DIY proves to be even more complex.

For example, how do you describe manual work and skills based on what is called "nonverbal experience"? As Jonas Frykman (1990: 50) and others have emphasized, the "silent knowledge" in people's lives cannot be transformed into text without losing important dimensions. How can we study something that is intangible and invisible? Words seem to be insufficient. You can also say the same about the roles of emotions in fieldwork.

In accomplishing DIY projects, you need to acquire a tacit knowledge that seems to reside in your body, as when you hit the nail with a hammer or choose the appropriate bits for the power screwdriver. You have to think ahead and plan your work. You must know what a circular saw is and how to use it. But you also do a lot of things without thinking consciously. It feels like the knowledge resides in your hands.

It is this tension or cooperation between hand and brain that I have become curious about. Now, when I swing the hammer or start the power saw, I am also looking at myself doing it and wondering about it. But when trying to reconstruct the processes of my different projects, it is easier to tell about *what* I did than *how* I did it. The gulf between words and actions is a constant challenge when writing about manual tasks.

DO IT BY FEEL

In the same way as I move between writing on the laptop and my DIY projects, I switch between thinking with tools and bodily movements, depending on the senses and tacit routines. How do you account for such alterations?

One way is to do as the sociologist Douglas Harper did (1987). For three years he observed, interviewed, and took many photos of Willie, an all-around craftsman in northern New York who, among other things, specialized in repairing old Saabs. Endless and very detailed descriptions of Willie's projects, in both his own words and as explained by Harper, give a profound account of this man's working knowledge, what he thought and what he actually was doing when repairing, grinding, and welding. In twenty pages, you get to know exactly how he built a stove door, redesigned a door handle, and so on. Yet many of these descriptions are hard to follow since they are rather technical, as in this extract in which Willie disassembles a Saab transmission:

> *When you reassemble it, you've got shim washers at the end of the shafts to make sure your bearings are seated right. Then your pinion shaft has a shim to make sure it sits out in the right position to hit the ring gear. It's a little more technical when you go putting them back together than it is taking them apart. Those gears have to all match up and run true. I do it by feel.* (Harper 1987: 124)

When I try to relate about my experience with tools and building materials, it is sometimes tempting to say, as Willie does, that I do it by feel. At other times, the things seem to become animated in their resistance or willingness to cooperate, as Jojada Verrips (1994) reports in his article "The Thing Didn't 'Do' What I Wanted It to Do!" It is as if they have an agency of their own.

What is it that I and other DIY people are doing, thinking, feeling, and imagining when we are working with tools and things? How are we learning to use appropriate devices and solve practical problems of different kinds?

WRITING DIY: THREE VERSIONS

In searching for answers to these questions, I shall try different ways of describing the project to make duckboards for the shower floor. In this experiment, I have been inspired by two examples. In his book *Exercises in Style*, the French author Raymond Queneau (1947) wrote ninety-nine retellings of the same simple story about a man with a long neck and a funny hat entering a crowded bus in Paris and having a short dispute with another passenger. The man then sees the same person two hours later at a train station getting advice on sewing a button to his overcoat. Each of these stories is written in a different style. For example, Queneau relates it as if it was a police record, a medical diagnosis, or a business letter. Other styles he uses are the meter of a sonnet, and rural nineteenth-century French. In this way, the author shows how one and the same event may be experienced and narrated in different ways, depending on the choice of words, symbols, and perspectives.

In another book, *A Thrice-Told Tale*, the anthropologist Margery Wolf (1992) uses three texts developed out of her research in Taiwan—a piece of fiction, anthropological field notes, and a social science article—to explore the same set of events. It was about a young mother who seemed to have lost her sanity and how her village neighbors reacted to that. In this case, Wolf demonstrates how different genres frame the three stories. A scientific text is expected to follow different rules from literary writing. The choice of style is based on the readers you are writing for—science colleagues from different disciplines or a nonacademic audience.

In her commentary on the three stories, Wolf discusses reflexivity, authorial presence, control, and the differences between fiction and experimental ethnography. She reflects on what her own personal and scientific background means in the fieldwork and in the writing. She is also thinking about her presence in the written text when she describes what she is doing and saying among the people she is studying.

As Wolf did, I shall write three types of small accounts about the making of duckboards: one specific, like a manual; one an informal and impressionistic story about a man called "George"; and one an analytic discussion of a more academic kind. How does the choice of style influence my way of thinking about this activity?

You may practice such experiments in order to develop your ability to observe and interpret social situations. You will then be reminded of how many different ways there are to describe an event or a phenomenon. Certainly it is you as a writer who chooses the style, the words, and the perspective. In this way, it is possible to say that you are in fact (re)creating the event.

Manual

At the timber yard, they proposed a water-repellent wood called "Cumaro" or "Brazilian teak," but it was rather expensive. My wife asked if I couldn't use some of the spruce wood I already had stored up. Of course, if they were made from spruce, these duckboards would not last as long as they would if they were made from a more water-hardy material. But if they rotted, I could just make new ones.

First I had to measure the floor in the bathroom with the folding rule. The area under the shower was 930 mm x 800 mm, and I decided to make the bars 50 mm wide, because I could then use boards that are 22 mm x 150 mm and make three lengths out of each with the circular saw. I fetched some boards that were planed on one side and laid them on a saw stand.

I made thirteen bars 50 mm wide and 910 mm in length. I also made four strips of the same wood as stringers to keep the bars together underneath. I

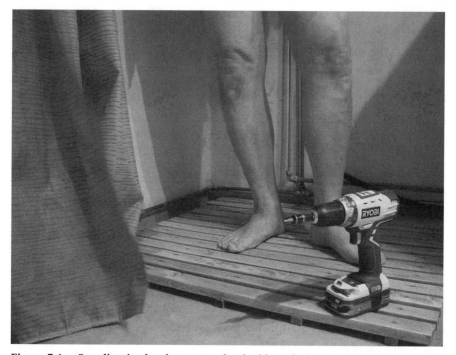

Figure 7.1.   Standing in the shower on the duckboards that you have made yourself is like reading a text that you have written. You may feel proud or look at it with critical eyes. What is the difference between the computer and the screwdriver in doing this type of work? (Billy Ehn)

filed and sandpapered the bars before fastening them with screws on the strips with 15-mm-wide openings. In the middle, I used the compass saw to make a hole for the washing machine hose (which we take away when the machine is off). The final task was to oil the duckboards several times.

Story

Without a do-it-yourself project on the go, George gets restless. When he had finished glazing the large veranda and making the guest house fit for winter living, there seemed to be nothing more to do. He felt empty. Luckily, his wife found out that they needed new duckboards for the shower floor in the big house. "Couldn't you make them?" she proposed, seeing him suffer. He immediately jumped on this idea.

As usual when doing carpentry, George didn't take notice of the time. With sweat in his eyes this sunny Saturday, he was in a joyful flow, with his heart in his work and completely occupied by interesting troubleshooting. He moved back and forth between meditative states and more-dramatic moments of activity. He felt like a moving and thinking part of the tools in his hands. Some of them, like the power screwdriver, the level, and the folding rule, were close friends in helping him to solve tricky problems. He was proud of mastering them, something he had learned late in life partly by observing his father-in-law in action.

It was both a serious and a playful task to make duckboards. The roaring circular saw plowed through the boards, the power screwdriver whirled dancing screws one by one down through the solid wood, and the sawdust filled the air like stinging insects. The sky was blue and the radio played Mozart. This radio, another essential device in George's DIY universe, was always on while he worked. So the experience of materials, tools, and bodywork was added to by a special piece of music or somebody talking, creating a special atmosphere.

It was a perfect day for outdoor work. The wind was sighing in the trees. The waves from the sea below the houses rolled calmly against the beach. Bent over the saw stand in his work clothes, totally immersed in the project, George felt as if he was a unity of body and mind, using the tools like musical instruments, not thinking of anything other than how to make fine duckboards.

The hands knew what to do, although his dexterity was not always perfect. He dropped things and fumbled with screws. Sometimes he was in too great a hurry, making errors that made him smile embarrassedly, relieved that no one else had seen them. You have to think before you start, he reproached himself. Measure twice, cut once! Sometimes, he used this internal monologue to remind him of what to do next. But mostly, the inner voice was silent, and then he was all eyes and body.

When the duckboards were completed, George showed the little masterpiece to his wife. She was very satisfied and, as she usually did when he had accomplished a DIY task, exclaimed: "Oh, how clever you are, George!" He was pleased, of course, but soon the feeling of emptiness returned. What to do next? He entered the carpenter's shed and looked urgently at the tools, as if they could suggest a new project.

Analysis

Studying DIY—making duckboards for the bathroom, for example—you realize that this is a social and cultural activity, even if you work alone. It is symbolically constructed, learned, and communicated. It is permeated by history, ideas, and values. In my case, I discussed the project with my wife. When I started up the circular saw to cut the wood into suitable lengths, I was reminded of her father, an autodidact himself, who had been my personal teacher in doing carpentry. He showed me how to "let the hammer do the work," by holding it right out on the handle, instead of in the middle. He also opened my eyes for the potential usefulness of so-called junk, all those things and materials that are hoarded up in the backyard or the cellar. I was close on his heels when he went to hunt for a piece of metal or a tube with the right dimension. In fact, being a self-taught person often means that you have learned a lot from others by watching them work in this way.

My father-in-law also gave me the circular saw and other tools that he no longer needs. These things are necessary, of course, for my DIY projects. But they have other meanings that are not always evident when using them (cf. Gauntlett 2011: 115). Besides containing ready-made answers to practical problems, they have involved me in different kinds of transactions, since I have bought them somewhere or received them from somebody. As Elizabeth Shove et al. (2007: 52) observe in a study of DIYers, gifts reveal personal histories of inheritance, exchange, gift giving, and attachment. They have a history connected to finished or unsuccessful projects and to situations when they have been broken or when somebody else borrowed them.

The tools require that you learn how to use them. This competence is at once embedded in humans *and* in things (Shove et al. 2007: 56). The combination of a person and a tool constitutes a human to nonhuman hybrid, or a "cyborg" (Haraway 1991). In this dynamic, skills and experience develop through using things. With a hammer or a power drill, you have other capabilities for engaging with reality than you do without them. The tools transform you, for example, into a potential carpenter, plumber, or electrician.

Another aspect of tools is their ability to communicate: when you hammer or start the circular saw, other people hear or see what you are doing. For example, when I made the duckboards, my wife and a couple of friends were watching me now and then from the veranda, where they were drinking coffee. When the circular saw got stuck and then jumped backward, one of the friends noticed; afterward, he told me it had looked dangerous. Even if actually there are no people looking at me when I am working, I sometimes imagine that there are, and that influences my behavior (cf. Goffman 1959).

We also have aesthetics. When I filed and sandpapered the bars and the strips, I wanted the surface to be soft and smooth to stand on in the shower. Many carpentry projects are guided, in the same way, by care for other people. The result will be nice to look at and will work well, of course. The question of aesthetics is often as crucial as the question of function (cf. Light and Smith 2005). Even if no one else notices my errors or my quick and dirty solutions, I may spend many hours redoing the work because I want it to be as perfect as possible. Sometimes you have to create optical illusions to hide irreparable errors. The look of the completed work, in this case the duckboards, becomes a mark of my identity as a carpenter.

WORKING KNOWLEDGE

These three ways of telling the story about the duckboards demonstrate different kinds of working knowledge. The first version is like a manual; you can use it for making duckboards yourself. In its exactitude, it is also a kind of bragging about my technical competence. The second account allows me to write about the emotions and sensuality that are involved in working with your hands. I use an alter ego to narrate this multisensory experience. The third text is very much like the rest of this chapter, using analytical concepts, generalizing, and referring to other researchers.

I enjoyed writing about George the most. I felt free to write what he felt and thought, as if I could read his mind. I really didn't make anything up, but followed my memory and imagination when choosing words and metaphors, picturing the situation rather than only using controllable facts. Writing the story helped me to see the inner life of DIY.

In an exercise like this, you can learn a lot from fiction writers, who, in their novels, use scene setting, overlapping dialogue, multiple points of view, composite characters, flashbacks, foreshadowing, interior monologues, and parallel plots. The point for an ethnographer in writing such narrative texts is that they make public what many researchers otherwise keep hidden: the private feelings, doubts, dilemmas, and uncertainties that confront the fieldworker.

But as I continued with the chapter, I left George and returned to the more conventional academic style of the third version, trying to sum up my main thoughts, as an ethnographer and cultural researcher, about DIY: the involvement, intimacy, intelligence, and sensuality that are brought to the fore when trying to solve practical problems.

Thinking further about switching between writing and manual work, I now see both differences and similarities. Unlike constructing duckboards, where picturing it in my mind I knew before I started what the product would end up looking like, I didn't know at all in advance what this chapter would contain; it is now, rather, a completely different text compared to the first draft of it. And unlike DIY, writing a text (for me) means writing several versions, deleting sentences and whole paragraphs, changing words, arguments, and even ideas. Making duckboards was a comparatively simple project, and I knew very well what the end product was. I saw it clearly; there it was, ready to be used, as it was intended. When writing, on the other hand, I have to discover the point, since it is rarely evident. There is more room for surprises when the reader takes over than when one places oneself on the duckboards.

As a carpenter you develop a sense of anticipation. You think ahead and visualize where you will end up, what you will do next, and follow that. When

I write, I first put together words to see what I'm thinking, and then I continue writing. If I have any preconception of where I will end up, it proves to be mostly wrong. The new version beats the old.

I almost always write something other than what I planned—and that is a blessing. It is the longing for discoveries that keeps me writing. Certainly, I "build" and "repair" my text, but I do these things without understanding much about the process. I feel that I have very little command of my thinking compared to when I'm using my recently acquired DIY expertise.

The building of a house may, of course, also implicate many changes and modifications, but it is a more linear process—notwithstanding all the minor and major errors, any nasty surprises, and anything else that goes awry. However, in spite of what I have just said, Elizabeth Shove et al. (2007: 61) believe there can be few DIYers who have completed a major project in exactly the way they anticipated, having gone through only the processes envisaged and using only the tools and materials they thought they would need. In that way, it once more resembles writing.

But even if DIY is almost inherently explorative, you don't suddenly decide to use bricks instead of wood for the walls. You may choose between screws and nails, but preferably you don't hit the nail with a screwdriver. You don't start out intending to make duckboards and end up with a firewood bin. And, again, it is easier to visualize the planned project. In DIY there are ready-made answers, but not in writing. Writing can take you almost anywhere, where it is even quite possible to hit metaphorical nails with a metaphorical screwdriver.

THE IMPORTANCE OF FAILURES

My description of writing about a DIY project might look rather simple. If so, it gives a wrong impression, as I think many other texts do. The finished and polished product often hides earlier mistakes and errors, which tend to get forgotten once the text is published.

Handling failures is an important part of ethnography and cultural analysis, as in all research. Working with a project or a paper may often be an activity with alternating highs and lows—a bad interview, no interesting observations, or a failed sweep on the Internet. However, when I talk to students, it is clear that writing is the research activity most strongly connected to feelings of disappointment and failure. There is the eternal problem of writer's block, with all kinds of helping hand tricks—from writing somebody an imaginary letter describing what you want to do to asking a friend to interview you about the study with the cell phone recording device on and turning the interview into text. These strategies emphasize the importance of choosing less anxiety-provoking forms of writing to get going.

It is fun to write when you sense the flow and your fingers are dancing on the laptop keys. You read what you have accomplished, and it looks wonderful. What good ideas and descriptions! You don't have to change one single word. (The next day you often think otherwise . . .) An outburst of self-confidence makes you blind to flaws.

But writing may, as I said, be a terrible experience, especially when you realize your own personal limitations when it comes to thinking and expressing your thoughts in a clear way. Self-censoring does not help you to be a productive writer. Reluctantly, you press the laptop keys and feel right away that this is not good at all. This experience makes you invent different kinds of excuses to avoid writing. You simply become afraid of it. How do you manage this fear?

In spite of having published many books and articles, writing this chapter meant tackling such problems even for me. In fact, it has been rewritten countless times during the last four years since the initial idea of writing about constructing my duckboards came to me.

Figure 7.2.   **As in ethnographic writing, when doing it yourself as an amateur carpenter, you have to be careful. The first few times you try to make something or write a text, you may feel clumsy and awkward. It's okay. Just do it again and again, until it works! (ThinkStock)**

One of the secrets of finally producing any kind of text is to have the courage to write badly in the beginning, allowing yourself to be naïve and clumsy—and then continue to revise your text, preferably with the helpful critique of other readers. This means that you have to stand the unpleasant experience of revealing your intellectual weaknesses, which are the root of your fear.

Weak self-confidence is easy to damage. Every failure in your text—from wrong spelling to theoretical incompetence—tells embarrassingly about your lack of ability. But, as was the case when, as an amateur carpenter, I made the duckboards, there is always the possibility of learning from your mistakes and developing your skills. Look at the first version of a chapter in your student essay as the lowest steps in a staircase. You have to pass them to get higher up; you can't reach the top in one move.

The fear of exposing your weaknesses should not prevent you from writing your deficient text, nor should it prevent you from showing it to a student friend or your supervisor. Consider their critique as a gift that will help you to produce a better essay. Hopefully, it will also make you a better writer next time. In any case, you, as well as I, need the critical and supporting eyes of friends and colleagues to make certain that your text is functioning.

WORKING AND WRITING

Working with the duckboards and this text has led me to reflect on three contrasting dimensions that I think are important for experienced researchers as well as essay-preparing students to consider.

First, in ethnographic writing, as in amateur carpentry, you are *mixing play and work*. Allow yourself to play and experiment with words and ideas, and do not always take it so seriously. You will then be better prepared for the business of producing scientific knowledge. You may work hard to express your ideas and find the "right words," but at the same time, you can let your mind wander and your imagination fly. Of course, you have to follow scientific rules, but that should not stop you from trying unconventional ways of thinking and writing. Almost anything is allowed if it develops an interesting text. It is the final and thoroughly edited version that counts.

Second, there are important *differences between discovering and representing*. In an earlier chapter, it was said that, for cultural researchers, writing is an essential part of the investigation; it is not just a way of reporting. This means that we treat words and sentences as research materials as well as the information and ideas that they are intended to convey. The words are, of course, used to represent (describe and interpret) reality, but they also are a reality in themselves: they *do* certain things; they have effects on both the writer and the readers.

Thinking through writing—or even writing before thinking consciously—means that you will get the opportunity to discover ideas that you didn't know you had, instead of only representing, or repeating, what you already know that you had thought. There is here, as I said before, a difference between carpentry and writing, since the latter may produce something different from what was planned. This makes you realize that research is rarely as rational as it is often portrayed in methodological handbooks.

Finally, you have to learn to *manage the personal and subjective dimensions in scientific writing*. Like the carpenter, the writer of a scientific text is using him- or herself in the work process—using the body, for example, and experiences, memories, expectations, and feelings. However, there is a temptation to hide this subjectivity in both crafting wood and crafting words, because it is connected with ideas of failure, bias, and unprofessional behavior.

But you don't have to surrender to that temptation. Instead of avoiding subjectivity, you should sincerely look your own person straight in the eyes. Who are you, producing these words and ideas? Which special resources and weaknesses have influenced your work? How can you use the knowledge about this in your next writing?

Studying my own manual labor, I had, in fact, rather poor control of the bias in the observations and interpretations resulting from my position as an elderly, white, privileged, academic male. These are only a few of all the potential social and cultural elements that influence the experience and textual representations of my carpentry.

Nowadays, after many years of discussions about reflexivity—as a way of analyzing the subjective aspects of the research process—it is common to hear that all social and cultural research, for better or worse, is predisposed in some way or other. Without bias—broadly defined here as "interest and commitment"—you perhaps cannot ask meaningful questions or look inquiringly at the world. Are there really any notions at all concerning human behavior and relations that are not preconceived?

Subjectivity should therefore not be seen as a threat to ethnographic detachment. Instead you should transform it into an analytic resource, by treating it in the same way as other people's subjective experiences. This means that the ethnographer will reflect on her or his fieldwork as being coproduced by those being studied. The lonely act of writing is consequently also a social and cultural act in which you communicate with real or imagined readers—as when I made duckboards for other people to stand on when having a shower.

8

DEMYSTIFYING FIELDWORK

Why do you teach people how to do ethnographic research by making them read ethnographies? Eating good food does not teach you anything about cooking. (Anonymous comment on a student evaluation)

In the 2003 film *Kitchen Stories*, Swedish efficiency researchers set out to study Norwegian men in their natural habitat. The sponsoring institute has strict rules about how the research is to be done with rigorous objectivity. The investigators live in small travel trailers next to the houses they are studying. They spend the day sitting in a high chair in a Norwegian's kitchen, watching and recording every action, never actually speaking to the person they are observing.

The comedy in the film emerges when one Norwegian study subject, Isak Bjørvik, starts watching his researcher, Folke Nilsson, through a hole in the floor. Eventually, the two men break out of their assigned roles and become friends, leading the audience to think about how ridiculous "objective" social science research can be, choosing to study humans in a way that is completely dehumanizing. But how much has social science really changed over the years that have elapsed since the 1950s, the setting of *Kitchen Stories*?

In the previous chapters we have discussed different research strategies, ways of searching for materials and bringing them into a dialogue. We have argued for a "bricolage approach" that reflects the radical changes ethnography and cultural analysis have undergone in later years. To understand this change, it is a good idea to see not only how traditional ways of doing fieldwork have been transformed but also how current styles of ethnography encompass much of a classic fieldwork approach. This traditional fieldwork attitude is present in many ways in modern ethnography, whether performed by anthropologists or European ethnologists, by cultural sociologists, or in the interdisciplinary field of cultural studies.

The argument of this chapter is also about the need to understand how the way you collect or produce material is shaped by routines and small rituals that are often perceived not as formal methods but as "the ways we do research

115

here" (in this special department, discipline, or generation). For example, you could apply the approaches, from earlier chapters, for studying invisible routines to your own research experiences, by comparing present styles of handling ethnographic information with the routines of an earlier era. You might find not only some striking differences but also some interesting similarities.

THE CLASSIC STYLE

Leaving the laboratory and the classroom for a place called "the field" to talk with real live people separated anthropology and European ethnology from other human sciences in the early twentieth century. Before this time, those interested in so-called primitive people got their information by corresponding with explorers and missionaries, quizzing colonial officials, and examining artifacts and skulls. Living people were even persuaded or coerced into going far off to spend time in universities and laboratories where they could be examined and studied.

The idea of leaving home for direct observation of people living in nature, and even talking with them, was radical and controversial. Early ethnographers concluded that the only way to get objective, comparable, and accurate information was to collect genealogies and folk tales directly from the people under study, learn their languages and customs, and bring home artifacts, notes, sound recordings, photographs, and even whole houses, boats, and temples. Over time the adventure of going to the field became a rite of passage for all aspiring ethnographers. Professors expected students to go find "their people" or "their village," learn the language and all the local customs, and then come home and write a book with a title like *The Nuer* or *The Kapauku Papuans*, including chapters titled "kinship and family," "religion and ritual," "politics," and the like.

You might think that going off to do an ethnography, being such an important way of turning a person into a professional, would require years of training and a lot of careful instruction by elders who had done it themselves. But you would be wrong. Instead students spent most of their time reading the ethnographies written by other people and almost no time at all learning the craft of ethnography. There were no courses or textbooks on how to actually go somewhere and do ethnographic research, beyond a strange and cryptic collection of lore called *Notes and Queries* (first edition 1874, sixth in 1951). Aside from the gossip they could pick up over drinks or at conferences, young anthropologists were sent off into the wilds to figure out how to do fieldwork on their own. Imagine trying to learn to cook by eating in restaurants where you were never allowed in the kitchen.

No wonder so many early ethnographies read like macho adventure stories where the lone ethnographer has to persevere and gradually learn through trial and error, eventually becoming accepted and even loved. Then the hero leaves "the field" and goes home to "write up." The main tools that ethnographers learned to use were the notebook and the typewriter, which were used to write something called "field notes." Alongside these formal notes, which were seen as a kind of official record, most ethnographers kept a journal or diary for their personal and private observations and feelings. The diary was the place for complaining about insect bites, inedible food, and annoying informants.

The Polish ethnographer Bronislaw Malinowski's diaries from his famous fieldwork between 1914 and 1918 in the Trobriand Islands of Melanesia were only published half a century later, and many anthropologists at the time were angry that his privacy had been violated. The venerated ancestor was revealed as "a crabbed, self-preoccupied, hypochondriacal narcissist, whose fellow-feeling for the people he lived with was limited in the extreme," according to the American anthropologist Clifford Geertz (1967).

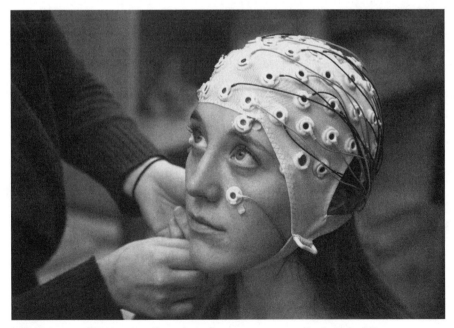

Figure 8.1.   Would we really want to measure someone's thoughts? In ethnography real human contact is the most important technique. (© by Susanne Ewert)

Fieldwork in the classic style was built on two formidable boundary-making distinctions. The first was between field and home: the place where information was "gathered" and the place where it became "data" and was transformed into a scientific document. The second division was equally important—the separation of the anthropologist him- or herself into two beings: the public recording scientist and the private human being living in a real and fragile body. This private being is dealing with the personal difficulties that are bound to happen when one is yanked out of one's home and thrust into a place he or she has never been. There, one usually has no friends or support system and is at the mercy of an alien and often unfriendly human and natural environment. Just like the character of Folke Nilsson sitting up in the high chair in Isak Bjørvik's kitchen, the anthropologist was supposed to keep the personal and the professional in two separate, sealed containers.

In retrospect, it is amazing that so many aspiring anthropologists survived fieldwork and made the passage back into being relatively normal college professors and professionals. As far as we know, nobody has counted up how many aspiring ethnographers actually fell by the wayside, casualties of an often cruel sort of initiation ritual. The classic model of ethnographic fieldwork was starting to crumble around the edges in the 1970s and 1980s, but most aspiring ethnographers were still expected to find a village or neighborhood somewhere and become fluent in the local language. They were supposed to become familiar with the ethnography of the larger region or country where their village was located so they could then present themselves on the job market as an "Africanist" or a "Caribbeanist," as if they had been branded by prolonged contact with the places they studied.

MAKING CHANGES TO THE CLASSIC MOLD

The world has changed a lot since the time of the classic lone anthropological hero who went off into the wilderness to bring back exotic tales. For one thing, it is getting very hard to find anywhere that is still isolated, unknown, and exotic. Reporters and self-styled explorers still manage to come up with some noncontacted tribe "still living in the stone age" now and then, but these usually turn out to be hoaxes.

More to the point, we have pretty much abandoned the idea that ethnography is a tool for white, educated European Americans to learn about the majority of "those others" out there. The globalization of knowledge and education has done a lot to change the context of ethnography. Anthropology and allied social sciences are now taught in universities and schools all around the world to people of many cultures. Even as early as the 1970s, anthropologists from Asia and Africa began to do pioneering fieldwork in Europe and North America, changing the geography of power and knowledge in a dramatic way.

New kinds of writing and expression flourish, and today, ethnographers are happily making documentary videos, recording the sounds of the forest at night, compressing their thoughts into haiku, and interviewing insects and fish. That is not to say that ethnographers are always writing good poetry or making entertaining and insightful films, but they are at least trying to find new audiences and present their ideas and experience in new and creative ways.

And the landscape of academic publication is changing by the month. New online journals are cropping up like weeds—some of them are reputable, and others are just pay-to-publish scams. The paper journals that used to fill the bookshelves of professors are rapidly disappearing, and the fate of the printed book is unknown. Some people are putting their notes and photos from field-work in locked file cabinets to protect anonymity, while others are document-ing their fieldwork in a series of unedited videos or in interactive discussions. In earlier chapters, we have seen how mobile technologies change the nature and rhythms of ethnographic research. Today, a single smartphone has all the tools that early ethnographers needed for their work, and it can also organize and transmit information in ways that Malinowski would have envied.

All of these new kinds of ethnography are built upon the ruins of the boundary between objective and subjective, ethnographer and "native." Once the researcher steps down from the high chair and sets aside the tools that keep him or her at a safe distance, enters the kitchen and talks with the cook, and even learns to cook and share a meal, ethnography becomes a kind of play-ground of possibilities. We can collaborate with the people we are studying, or work for them on contract, or even share with them the responsibility for defining our research goals and methods. And moving away from the classic notion of studying an exotic culture has finally allowed us to begin looking at our own lives in new ways. Many ethnographers are now quite happy to shed their science costumes—their white lab coats—and the straightjacket of rigid methodology. It often feels liberating to write in different voices and speak to different audiences.

However, there is a price to be paid for leaving our high chair of objec-tivity. Science has an undisputed authority in the world, built on the fruits of technology and successful explanation of otherwise mysterious phenomena. Once, a student challenged a professor of biological anthropology with the popular notion that "science is just another worldview." The professor turned to the board and drew a mushroom cloud, and then turned back and said, "Maybe so, but it is the only worldview that can blow up the planet."

This is an important point. Science has power in the world, and many social scientists worry that giving up objectivity, standards of measurement, and mathematical language leaves ethnographers with no authority to speak in public about policy and key issues. These are essential issues that have no simple solution. One response among ethnographers has been to pay a great deal more attention to their methods and to how anthropologists might lay claim to "truth."

THE JUNGLE IDEAL

One way to explain how technology and new media have changed ethnographic fieldwork is to trace my own practices since I (in this chapter, Richard Wilk) started my dissertation fieldwork in Belize in 1979. At first, my experience followed the classic ethnographic voyage of exploration into the "heart of darkness." I worked with indigenous people in the rain forests of southern Belize, the most remote part of the most remote district, with people who, up to that time, had been little studied.

One of the first villages I worked in required a long drive down muddy and rutted roads to a small town, a terrifying ride on the ocean and up a river in a dugout canoe, and an arduous half-day hike on muddy trails over jagged hills. I worked in a foreign language, lived in a thatched hut, and, once a month, went to town to collect mail and make a few phone calls through a noisy line. The surroundings were so new, every day was full of discoveries, but I was also missing my friends and family, my home, and all my familiar daily routines, my clothing and food.

Because everything was new, I took notes on everything, in my typed field notes and by hand in a series of field journals, where I also made sketches, wrote bad poetry, and pasted interesting documents. Another important part of writing was the letters I sent to my girlfriend and to friends and family. My biggest problem was that there never seemed to be any time when I was *not* doing ethnography. I woke up with curious little faces of children peering through the sticks that formed the walls of my house, and they spied on me when I went to the river to bathe or into the bushes to defecate.

Because I was interested in agriculture and productivity, I asked farmers to record for me, every week, how many hours they worked. I visited cornfields and estimated the harvests based on traditional measures. I did censuses to find out who were living and working together. I interviewed farmers about all the varieties of crops, took part in community rituals from funerals to costumed dances, and learned how to build houses, burn limestone into quicklime, hunt, and fish.

I used a cassette recorder to record stories, long meetings, and complicated conversations, which I could translate and transcribe later, and I usually carried a pen and a small pad for notes. I had a notebook for my maps and notes when I was mapping fields and villages, a card file for everyone's name and kinship relationships, a sheaf of survey forms for my household census, and my field notebooks where I sketched and kept my personal reflections. A calendar on the wall recorded major events, rainfall, floods, and my trips in and out of the village, and I wrote long letters to my advisor and to friends describing my fieldwork experiences. I kept notes on all the articles and books I had taken with me to the field as well, notes which seemed somehow out of place in my field notes, but I did not have anywhere else to put them.

The only times I was "off duty" were the quiet night hours after the rest of the village was asleep, when I sat up typing my field notes and swatting the flies attracted to my kerosene lantern while listening to the BBC news on a shortwave radio. Even leaving the village for a trip to town was no relief—I was still observing, taking notes, and using my camera and tape recorder in an alien place. Fieldwork ended only when I left Belize and went back to graduate school in Arizona; I took "my data" back so I could start a phase called "analysis," followed by a long time when I did almost nothing beyond writing and sending out job applications. The entire project did not culminate until six years after writing the dissertation, when I finally published a book based on my fieldwork.

I should mention that by the time I went to the field, I had been told many times about ethnographers who had lost all their notes by leaving them on a bus or in a car that was stolen. To make sure this did not happen to me, I used carbon paper in my typewriter to copy each page of notes, and every month I would send the copies back to my dissertation advisor.

It is amazing how durable this model of research has been in anthropology, even though the actual working lives of most ethnographers are very different. Today you are more likely to find an anthropologist working in a hospital, a government office, or a genetics laboratory than to find them tromping around the jungle or the distant countryside. Even if "anthropology at home" is dominating the field, there is still a lingering jungle ideal. To do research, you have to go "out there" in order to be welcomed back into the fold as a professional. I will return to this issue later.

WHERE IS THE FIELD NOW?

That boundary between *home* and *field* that once defined the work of ethnographers has become much harder to find since I did my first fieldwork in Belize. Ethnography itself has been adopted by many different disciplines from education to consumer research. This means that for some people, the field has become the classroom itself, threatening the boundary between teaching and research. Aren't teachers engaged in a kind of applied research when they give tests and grade papers? They are trying to find out what students have learned, how much they have retained from readings, lectures, and discussions.

While anthropologists and ethnographers were busy writing methodology textbooks about the joys and perils of fieldwork, the world was changing. The growth of the Internet, cheap and durable computers, and a whole host of other new information technologies made the concept of fieldwork mutate and gradually dissolve. We no longer know exactly where the field is, and work itself has been redefined in fundamental ways. Either fieldwork has expanded to take over our entire lives, or perhaps it is the other way around. Technology has entered everyday life in new ways, so that we always seem to be multitasking. It is also often asserted that social media are changing people's conceptions of relationships and that they even are turning common life into a kind of mass-media performance.

The most important change is perhaps the way e-mail, Skype, and other communication tools have made new kinds of "fieldwork" possible. Working in southern Belize used to be like living on another planet—it took weeks for mail to arrive, and you had to reserve a public phone to make a call, and then wait while an operator connected you, while you sat in an airless little booth.

Today I can e-mail the children and grandchildren of the people I interviewed where I did my first fieldwork, and on a good day, I can do a video call on Skype. Some anthropologists now do all their research through the Internet, including interviews and surveys. In my last book on Belize, I had a small group of readers on a Belizean bulletin board who would read sections of the work and point out my mistakes. Several times, I asked the group questions, and parts of their answers went right into the book. It really makes no difference if I am e-mailing a Belizean in Belize, or in Chicago or L.A., which now have sizable Belizean populations. One of my students did her dissertation research in the Belizean community in Chicago. Another married a Belizean and now has homes and families in both countries. I have had Belizean students in a class at my own university. So where is "the field" now?

The revolution in computing and recording technology has made many kinds of traditional methods for preserving interviews, notes, photographs, videos, and other kinds of information completely obsolete. As more forms of information become digital, we can keep and analyze many in the same platforms, and this makes coordination and linking of different evidence much easier. Programs like Nudist and AskSam allow you to identify themes and organize all your documents for easy retrieval.

In the analog age, when I took a picture, I would record the date and the subject in a little notebook, and weeks or months later, I would write codes on every slide. Then I had to leaf all through my interview transcripts and field notes, and write a cross-reference to the photographs in the margin, by hand. Now linking photos to text is simple, because both are digital and both are on the same computer. My audio recordings of songs, comments, interviews, and radio programs also required a little log book, so I would know what was on each tape and could link it to field notes again with little notes in the margins of typed pages. If I transcribed an interview, that created another thing that had to be manually catalogued and linked. It was a nightmare, and I often found myself spending an hour just trying to find the right tape, and then figuring out where a particular recording might be on that tape.

Back in the days of pens and notebooks, there was a clear separation between fieldwork and library research. Early on in the process of formulating and writing a proposal, and then later while writing up the results, a scholar was expected to go to the catalogues and shelves in a university library, to take out a bunch of books and consult the heavy tomes of bound journal issues, taking notes with a pen in a notebook. By 1990, hand scanners for copying printed text were available, and as OCR technology advanced, new ways of copying text and bibliography made library and archival research much easier. Today, a digital camera or a cell phone can effectively scan any text it is aimed at, and bibliography programs have eliminated a lot of the work of keeping track of references and footnotes, which used to be a time-consuming chore, just like drawing graphs and illustrations in the predigital age.

ORGANIZING INFORMATION

If getting enough "data" was hard for earlier ethnographers, today the problem is more likely to be too much data, too many hyperlinks, and an endless trail of web pages that are full of information of varying (and often unpredictable) reliability. The abundance of sources for information has obliterated the division between "field" and "library" research, given that many of us have not physically entered a library in years. In a single day, it is not unusual for me to find websites, references, photos, quotations, e-mails, and web links that are connected to one or more of the dozen "open" projects I am working on, or to lectures and presentations, or to a discussion with a colleague, or to advising my students, or that may provide interesting or funny things to pass along to friends and family.

While getting information used to be the main task of the ethnographer, today we teach ethnography in a world saturated with text, audio, and video, and the major analytical task is organizing and prioritizing, making categories and connections. This entails figuring out where to put things and being able to find them later.

I started out on computers, when we still used eighty-column IBM punch cards, and since then I have moved my data to nine-track tapes on reels, 5-inch floppies, 3.5-inch disks, then zip-drive cassettes, CDs, and now DVDs, hard drives, as well as in the "cloud" in various places. The first useful analytical software was SPSS (Statistical Package for the Social Sciences) on the mainframe, with Unix-based programs on a minicomputer, then Database II, III, and IV, and other orphan tools like Reflex on a personal computer, and now to Atlas TI and a variety of Excel spreadsheets. I have no electronic versions at all of documents I wrote before 1989, and many of the early ones are in extinct word-processing formats like Sprint, WordStar, and WordPerfect.

Today, an ethnographer just starting off needs to think forward to all of the kinds of information that will form part of a future life and career, and to think about how that information can be preserved and indexed in a way that is likely to be viable in twenty or thirty years. My advice would be to stick to the most common software tools, which have open and widely used file types, like "txt" and "doc" files, "pdfs," "mp3s," and "jpgs." It is more likely that future formats will be backward compatible, and you will not have to laboriously convert one kind of data into another. Also be wary of any indexing or analytical tool that requires you to change your existing files into another format that the program will read, because it might become a "dead end" if the software company dies or is swallowed up by another.

This is why I recommend using tools that can read and organize many different kinds of data in their native formats or that make it easy to move back and forth between the two. Right now, I use two kinds of programs that allow me to find what I need among my tens of thousands of files, and organize new stuff into folders that are flexible and make sense. The first is a straightforward (and free) indexing application called Copernic Desktop that reads every word, using Boolean operators like "and" and "or" to allow you to find particular phrases or passages.

While I am transcribing an interview in MS Word, I can add codes that relate to every theme in my project. Then, when I want to see all the documents on a single topic, I can just search for those codes. I can also put those codes in the file names of photos or other graphics and videos. It is simple and quick, and it allows me to go back and add or change index terms when new topics or themes pop up. The only drawback is that it only indexes text and file names; it cannot index photos, video, or audio except by their titles. Both PC and Mac worlds have built-in indexing software, though they are often clumsy and hard to use.

Figure 8.2.   Try sitting at a table in a city café for half an hour and writing down everything you see. But you cannot record even a tiny fraction of what is going on. What should I look at, what should I describe? Doing ethnographic observations is always about choosing: selecting focus, perspective, questions, and words. (Billy Ehn)

Then there is a second kind of organizing task. Where do you want to keep personal documents like poems, diaries, angry letters to the local newspaper, wedding vows, articles about headache cures, and receipts for repair work done on your house foundations? You may also have to save receipts for school and personal books, some of which might be tax deductible. What do you do with inspiring bits of text that you want to keep but don't know if and when you will want to use in the future?

Is it "research" if you get a good idea from reading a science fiction or mystery novel in your leisure time, and where do you keep your random brainstorms? How about the funny pictures you find on the web that you want to hold on to, or the pictures of meals you have eaten or cool menus—important if you are a food scholar. If you try to just bookmark things, you will often return to find the link doesn't work anymore. The average life span of a web page is somewhere between forty-four and seventy days, and at any time, more than half of all hyperlinks are invalid (statistics from Google).

At this moment, my favorite tool for keeping all the shards of my digital life organized and retrievable is freeware called Evernote; it gives you many ways to keyword or index your documents, and to keep photos and other data organized. You can snap something with your phone or camera, and Evernote will convert any words in the picture into searchable text. It can also georeference locations for pictures, and there is an extension for recording pictures of meals for the food-obsessed ethnographer. The database resides in the cloud, so it is accessible from anywhere with the Internet, and there are versions for most smartphones as well. Within a few years, we expect a full suite of ethnographic apps will be available.

None of these tools does the specialized work of keeping track of bibliography, a major task, given the boom in both online and paper publications in academia. There are several good add-on programs for MS Word, but my current choice is Zotero, another free program that will copy references from almost anywhere on your screen and put them instantly into any format you might want. The most important thing as you begin your career as a student or researcher is to find one bibliography program and stick with it; in the future you are never going to go back and start entering hundreds of references you kept in other programs or documents.

The question all scholars will have to face in the future is this: How do you keep your public face separate from your private life? Do you believe that all data shall be free, or do you think you have a right of possession over the things you write? Because all kinds of information is becoming publicly available on the Internet, you are going to be faced with some tough choices about how you are going to present your work and what kinds of things you want to keep private. The division between the personal and the professional is just as tenuous as the difference between public and private; my Facebook page is a tablet open to friends who know nothing about anthropology and to my family members who might not admire my profession. I have been trying to make my papers and book reviews available for free on my academia.edu page, but why would anyone want to buy my books if they can find them for free on a Chinese bootleg website?

PAST, PRESENT, FUTURE

What can be learned from this academic journey? There are parallels here to the comparisons between analog and digital generations in chapter 5, "Do You Remember Facebook?" Every academic generation—whether in the 1880s or the 2010s—tends to see its own life history as revolutionary because it has encompassed so many dramatic changes. Sometime in the future, when you look back at your student years in the 2010s, there will probably be both nostalgia and wonderment. "Do you remember how we did research back then, using gadgets like laptops and small cameras inserted into cell phones?"

For this book, we interviewed colleagues and students about their everyday research routines. Several things were striking. First of all, there is a strong sensual dimension worth exploring further: "I just love that warm light of the computer screen, asking me to start writing" or "I just can't work only on the screen. I need to print out stuff, find a good chair, and sit down with a pencil and cup of coffee. I must feel the papers in my hand"; or "Sometimes I spread out my text draft on the floor. It is great to be able to walk along neat rows of paper, suddenly seeing my text materialized in space." People mix analog and digital tools, because they do different things to materials, ideas, and writing. Post-it notes surround computer screens; home pages are turned into printouts.

Research is very much about not only the movement of ideas and texts but also the constant handling of research stuff. Movement does something not only to the material but also to the researcher. People told us how they choose different spots for work, in the wonderful silence of the home, the hushed bustle of a library, or the stimulating buzz of a café.

Second, people create their own special order and work routines. Just look at tidy or messy work desks or peep into the laptop inventories of others. A colleague remembered how her move to a new office had catastrophic consequences. "I tidied up everything, put stuff in binders, and started out with a clean desk. Then I found out I couldn't work in this environment, it was all too neat and orderly. I had to re-create the mess of my old office." A computer desktop or hard drive can reflect a similar kind of chaos, where files are scattered at random and one can never find the latest version of a document.

Third, throughout this book we have argued that research goes on all the time; new ideas and materials appear in all kinds of situations. We found, however, that some students questioned if they really did serious research: "I don't feel like a real scholar when I am just out surfing the Net," one of them complained and invoked a nostalgic image of traditional research, with white coats in the lab, fieldwork in small villages, or backs bent over documents in the sacred stillness of the archive.

Back in "those days" research took place in a distinct manner, with analog materials stored in boxes, in files, and on shelves, or pinned to walls. How is this compared to just sitting at home clicking one's way through cyberspace? Another student put it like this: "Why is it that I often feel like I am cheating when I race through the Net in search for references or good quotes?" What they forget, of course, is that research practices tend to look more orderly in retrospect, while the present always seems messy and unfinished. Analog search methods like letting the finger glide along book spines in the library or asking colleagues for references created certain search routines. Today, the Internet offers sources and materials that earlier generations could only dream of.

There is something disturbing about the way the new environment we work in is constantly bombarding us with information, images, thoughts, music, and jokes. Some of this might be useful, but we need some way to catch the useful pieces and put them away in our extended memory so that we will find them again.

It is important, however, to remember that research is very much about selecting and deselecting. Learning to ignore, forget, and overlook is the other side of focusing. Without those skills we would constantly drown in materials and ideas. The skill of ignoring things must constantly be trained in order to prevent paper writing or thesis work from overflowing. At every stage of the research process, there is the need to abstain from certain paths, materials, or issues.

The skill of ignoring is only one of the many research routines that we use but seldom think about. People create their own research strategies and constantly acquire new skills, such as navigating through potential material and making split-second decisions about what seems worth noticing. There is a slowly accumulated competence of cutting corners, skimming, and skipping, knowing which e-mails to answer and which memos to read, and judging a book by holding it in one's hand. Although such routines may be experienced as very personal, they are intensely cultural products of a socialization into values, conventions, and unspoken rules in specific academic settings and different research paradigms.

Questions of power and authority enter here. Who is allowed to cut corners, skim a text, or develop more laid-back or bohemian routines in selecting and deselecting academic information? What kinds of research routines can a graduate student, an untenured lecturer, or an old professor get away with?

Power dimensions are also found in the ways changing aesthetic values influence research and writing habits: a nice printout, a beautiful argument, a good looking diagram, a well-balanced text, a scholarly approach, a pleasing order, or a creative disorder in the office. The historical perspective illustrates how scholars learn to mix or switch between available microgenres. The post-it note, the e-mail, the footnote, the text message, the observation protocol, the field notes, and the conference paper all call for different styles of writing, framed by cultural conventions that change over time and between academic settings.

Talking about changing research techniques and tools may overemphasize the element of newness. Looking at different academic generations, the strong continuity is also striking. In some ways, doing ethnography and cultural analysis of the everyday has a stubborn persistence, which might be difficult to spot. We could call it "the fieldwork attitude," which lives in jungle fieldwork as well as in netnography. It consists of keeping an open and curious mind, ready to search for ideas and materials in all kinds of strange places.

An ethnography is always something like a magic trick where "information" is held up in the hand and then in a flash, the hand is holding up a finished essay or book. Through examples, the other chapters in this book show you what is behind the magical appearance; it is often hard and challenging work that it is sometimes serendipitous. Some people may have a lot more aptitude for this kind of work than others have. There is no way to discover your own skills without trying them out. You have to be ready to take advantage of any little opportunities, like cracks in the facade, that may give insight. Sometimes it comes in a flash, but more often, it requires us to go back through our notes, records, photos, and other ephemera we might collect, like used train tickets or the rotted wood slats from the shower. These are all part of our living museum of memory, traces of our past perceptions and thoughts.

9

TAKING CULTURAL ANALYSIS OUT INTO THE WORLD

As fieldworkers, we focus on the everyday life of ordinary people. We explore what they are interested in and what they value, but also things that are unconscious or forgotten. We see whole situations where others see fragments. We put trends, patterns of behavior, and changes in lifestyles in a new light. With cultural analysis we promise something different, a new angle, another perspective, making the invisible visible or the inconspicuous important.

This is a former student talking about her job as a trend analyst. We had asked her what use she had made of her academic training. What happens when you take ethnography and cultural analysis out into the world?

In this final chapter, we will address life after university. Some students will continue doing cultural analysis inside academia, but most will be working elsewhere. How can you use what you have learned about ethnographic methods in studying, for example, family meals or DIY activities, and analyze them in cultural terms, when you take up jobs outside of the university?

We interviewed former students, such as the one quoted above, about their first experiences as interns and their early jobs, but we also talked to those who have a long experience of putting their knowledge to work. We found that students with training in cultural analysis often ended up in jobs that they hadn't thought of as possibilities when they began their studies.

Some became involved in urban planning and public welfare policy, or worked with issues of cultural diversity. Some formed their own consultancies offering their services to both corporate clients and public organizations. Others became members of corporate research teams in product development, marketing, or management. Their employers or clients could be anything from a small NGO outfit or a local town council to large government agencies and global corporations. Wherever they ended up, they always found uses for the skills they learned in studying ethnography and cultural analysis, in forging their careers. Their training also made them flexible, creative, and highly adaptable. There are many examples in the contributions to the *Handbook of Anthropology of Business* (Denny and Sutherland 2014).

THE SURPRISE EFFECT

There are some uniting themes that emerge from all these varied occupational fields. What do employers and clients want from cultural analysts? First of all, they want something different from what they get from traditional research methods such as consumer surveys or focus group interviews. They want to be surprised and to learn something new that still makes sense. They also like the idea of doing ethnography, which has lately become a buzzword full of potential. Ethnography carries a promise of something more colorful and experimental. There is also a magic in "fieldwork," actually getting out into the urban jungles, talking to people, observing people in the mundane routine of daily life.

Cultural analysis is sometimes called "the serendipity approach," because a researcher may not actually know what to look for when beginning a study. Such a label, however, may hide the cumulative and systematic dimensions of analytical work, which only *appears* to be anarchistic. Although fieldwork may appear to be a very improvised and informal activity, it calls for a constant and critical reflexivity about preconceived notions or prejudices, rather than building those assumptions into the research design at the beginning. That is a procedure that ensures that the research will confirm what is expected. In contrast, cultural analysis seems vague and open, and you never know where it might end up. Some academics and clients find this disorienting. Is this really research?

When marketing their special skills, cultural analysts will, as in our opening quote, have to prove that their methods produce new and different kinds of knowledge. Consultants thus constantly have to demonstrate that ethnography is good for reaching those "aha!" insights that are so often missing in conventional studies. This often calls for challenging the preferences for quantitative data collection that are found among many employers. "One of the things we learned early was to argue for the potentials of a qualitative approach," a consultant ethnographer remembered. "Our clients at first found it hard to understand why ten in-depth interviews could produce more interesting knowledge than a 'scientific sample' of forty quick ones."

Consultants learn to argue against the wisdom of market surveys or preconceived ideas about what customers want or need. Often you end up finding things that neither you nor your clients had anticipated. One of the practical purposes of this method is that designers, communicators, and product de-

Figure 9.1.   Taking cultural analysis out into the world means being ready to investigate anything from a cultural point of view. How do you interpret this mundane street scene from Lisbon, Portugal? Discuss your thoughts with others and you might discover how subjective your perception is. (Billy Ehn)

velopers will understand the relationship between what they produce and the meanings the products and messages have for the audience and users.

OPEN FIELDWORK

The expanding interest outside of academia in ethnography and cultural analysis is thus a reflection of the demand for knowledge about the more qualitative aspects of everyday life. As we have argued in this book, qualitative work has the time to notice the importance of the small things, of emotions, tastes, and atmospheres.

A former student who was employed by a large manufacturer of household appliances found herself in a traditional industrial setting, where engineers and product developers usually devised new products drawing on their own experiences or with the help of some market surveys. She had been hired as an ethnographer to study the practices of so-called user-driven innovation.

She began by exploring the needs, interests, and priorities found in the everyday lives of potential customers. This called for a much more open kind of fieldwork, which challenged many of the routines of product developers. For example, she documented preparations for a weekend party in four families in different national settings. How do you turn your home into a setting ready to be inspected by guests—by cleaning, tidying, and rearranging? Her investigation made her employers look at their products with new eyes.

Other former students remember being thrown into instant work demands that they did not feel properly prepared for:

> *I'll never forget my first internship day, working for a consultancy firm. I was expected to do an ethnography of a suburban setting that was about to be re-branded. In the evening I got a call from my new boss saying "Are you ready to start tomorrow morning? I'll drop by your apartment tonight and give you a video recorder and some instructions."*
>
> *After an hour he appeared and called me to come down to his car. He was so stressed and just gave me a couple of quick hints and handed over the camera. "Are you ready to go ahead?" he said and what could I answer but a faint "yes." Next day I went out there and tried to remember my training in ethnography, finding out what to look for. I was just thrown right into it.*

Even if this particular student, and others, felt as if they were "thrown right into it," they usually managed to improvise and accomplish their tasks. Their education in ethnography had prepared them for the unexpected and the irregular, and had taught them to be flexible and use the tools that are available. They knew that there is not just one established way to seek knowledge.

WHAT'S THIS THING ABOUT CULTURE?

For many students, it is still a bit of a culture shock to take on their first projects in new settings. One student was on an internship with a big utilities company. He will never forget the first comment he received when he was presenting his project to his new colleagues. His aim was to do a cultural analysis of how the customers viewed the company that provided electricity for domestic use. "Culture? Damn it, we don't deal with culture here, we sell electricity!"

He had to explain what he meant about cultural analysis, and he talked about the reactions to the company he had encountered from customers; about the undecipherable complex monthly bills, for example, that they opened with trembling hands during the cold and expensive winter months. He realized that his next task was to elaborate on the many cultural charges found in an intangible product like electricity—a basic, invisible element in everyday life often surrounded by conflicts in the household. Who forgot to turn off the light again, and who is constantly fiddling with the thermostat? How do people work out how much long showers, open windows, or washing the dishes is costing them? Questions about waste and thrift, saving pennies, or battling global warming were often part of their thinking about energy. Electricity turned out to be a commodity framed by some very different cultural understandings, conventions, and moral norms.

Other interviewees talk of similar challenges. They had to try to get their employers or clients to understand the "cultural" part of cultural analysis. The arguments they used in the seminar rooms did not usually work. One had to find new ways of getting the message across. What is it that I have to offer? What are my competences and analytical skills? What is the ethnographic contribution to business studies, and what happens if we look at a phenomenon in terms of "culture": an office setting, an urban traffic situation, or a visit to the supermarket, for example?

One former student became involved in a project on waste management and found that the engineers she was going to work with looked puzzled when she said that "waste is very much about culture." She convinced them of this by doing a quick project in which a group of students with diverse cultural backgrounds were asked to label and sort different kinds of food waste. Faced with empty bottles, food leftovers, pizza packages, orange peels, how did they decide what should go back into the fridge or into the kitchen's system for sorting garbage? Gradually she convinced the engineers that waste reflected basic cultural ideas of value, order, and power, as well as having strong emotional charges. Those moments of breakthrough, when the client finally understands, are immensely gratifying to the researcher.

A DOUBLE CULTURAL ANALYSIS

High self-esteem is obviously necessary in this world. But it is not enough to propagate your competence and convince the clients you are worth every penny. You also have to "learn their language and move around in different settings like a chameleon—without giving up your individual character," as one of the consultants said. Meeting the world of business or public sector administrators also means running into their stereotypes of researchers, or as another interviewee put it:

> I usually dress up a bit and then tell my audience, "Did you expect me to turn up with a ponytail and a baggy sweater?" Their laughter tells me that this is precisely what they had expected.

One of the implications of this adaptation to a new world, be it a corporation, a public institution, or an NGO, is that you will find yourself doing a kind of double research. First you have to learn the culture of your client, and then you go out and do the study for which you are ostensibly getting paid. The final stage of research is no longer just producing a paper or report; now it means presenting your results, often to a skeptical audience. A flair for drama or comedy can be very useful at this point.

Understanding how the client sees the world is important. One of the former students told about her first project, which started out as a real failure. She was supposed to do an evaluation of an NGO project for bringing immigrant youths into the labor market by offering them computer training. Everything was prepared: student volunteers stood ready as mentors for the teenagers, a big computer company donated equipment, and a public housing company had fixed up facilities for "Internet cafés" out in the suburbs. But no clients arrived. What was wrong? The evaluator soon realized that this well-intentioned project was based on a false assumption about the young people they wanted to reach, who were actually as computer literate as any normal teenagers and had no desire to learn the drudgery of word processing.

The new Internet cafés, which had been opened with festive celebrations, remained empty, but when the evaluator met the project leaders, they did not want to hear her criticisms. Was the reason for this failure a lack of preparation and a false view of the realities? "I learned one thing in an instant," she said. "Never try to be the *besserwisser* (smart ass) and present an evaluation that can be read as an accusation. It will get you nowhere." It could not be admitted that this whole project, on which so much money and effort had been spent, was founded on a basic error, so instead they defended it against the cultural insights voiced by the researcher.

The evaluator realized that she had to change perspective and try to understand why her clients found her findings and recommendations so threatening. Her job was not to criticize this project and pull it apart, but to try to save what could be saved and help to organize a relaunch of it. Again, she had to analyze not only the teenagers she was set to study but also her clients' ways of thinking and acting.

There are many examples of this need for understanding a new job setting. Another intern remembers how forlorn she felt at first. People were stressed and showed very little interest in her.

That's when I decided to make a quick cultural analysis of the work place in order to learn how I could work my way into this tight-knit community. I started mapping routines and rituals in the office. What were the important social situations? The coffee break, of course, so I volunteered to take care of that daily ritual. Next I looked

at the internal networks and figured out how I could be part of them. Soon I became
both known and accepted.

LEARNING TO COMMUNICATE

Students, moving between the different worlds of academia and business, also had to learn how to present the knowledge they have produced. Success is very much about communicating to different audiences. It could be nurses who want new perspectives on caring for the elderly, producers of vacuum cleaners who need to know what counts as "dirt," or urban planners who want to understand the mechanisms behind growing segregation in the city.

"It is not at all like writing an essay," a student remembered from his first job following the reorganization of a social security agency. "I produced a fifteen-page report and they asked me to go home and turn it into a two page presentation with smart bullet points."

The lessons to be learned concerning communication are important, since a common complaint we meet among students is that they lack confidence in their skills as cultural analysts or don't know how to present those skills in simple words. Coming from the humanities where there is not much of a tradition of assured self-presentation, students are often insecure: What do I know? What kinds of competences do I have compared to an economist, a law student, or a hands-on engineer? Why should I be hired? There is so much that you have learned that you are not even aware of as being analytical skills or assets.

In this regard, you have much to learn from experienced professionals, both about the capabilities your education has given you and which new competencies you need to acquire. There is an abundant literature about the practical know-how needed to succeed as a cultural analyst in different work settings, and much concrete advice. One hands-on approach is provided by two American anthropologists who were also private consultants for many years, Carla N. Littlefield and Emilia Gonzalez-Clements (2008). They discuss how to start and operate a consulting business. For example, they say that the consultant must be a master of multitasking and keeping track of details, including keeping a schedule and being on time. "Cold calls" should not be seen as failures, but as lessons in rejection. You also have to learn how to price your service, promote your company, and start networking to find clients. This is something you can learn from earlier generations of students who are already out there.

Another necessary skill is the ability to communicate your results in a way that catches the attention of the client. You have to be lucid and know how to summarize, one of the former students said. It's forbidden to present your research in a way that is too abstract and complicated. The reports have to be short, clear, and easy to read, containing direct answers to the questions of the employer, without scientific references and methodological expositions. Concentrate on the most important things.

It works well to tell arresting stories, another interviewee said, to talk in metaphors, show images, and use PowerPoint. The language should not be "academic," yet it should be professional and qualitative. Visual images are important. "Sometimes, we spend a lot of time finding the perfect video clip that will bring out the core of our argument," as one professional put it. Others have learned that doing something unexpected will attract attention, like presenting a couple of material objects to illustrate the main idea, for example. "Our audience soon forgot most of our PowerPoint message, but they remembered the interesting stuff we put on the table." Again, don't overlook the importance of small things in gaining and demonstrating insights into cultural patterns and processes.

TIME DISCIPLINE AND TEAMWORK

In contrast to academic research, which often is rather slow and painstaking, applied cultural analysis is said to be very fast. You do not have months and years to sit down and think about the complexity of your material. The employers and the customers are in a hurry and expect speedy research and lucid results. In a short time you have to make yourself acquainted with a new and often strange context, and at the same time you must be cautious and avoid making premature conclusions.

But compared to the ordinary world of business, you are still working in a slower tempo. For example, the consultants among the interviewees often use two to three months to reflect on problems that the customers usually want to solve at once. The time constraints make it necessary to develop skills of tight budgeting of time and resources. Working with an eight-week assignment means that you constantly have to think about priorities and keep deadlines—it becomes a highly disciplined kind of investigation.

To get the most out of these conditions, you have to be creative in combining bits of preliminary observations with team-based brainstorming sessions, with walls cluttered with yellow post-it slips or mind maps drawn on the whiteboard. There is a movement back and forth between reflections, collection of new materials, swapping crazy ideas, and disciplining chaos into a finished project. What kinds of fieldwork should you do?

Figure 9.2.   Anything that strikes you as odd or out of place can be an invitation to explore culture. (Richard Wilk)

How about, for example, following a man on parental leave for a full fortnight, observing and discussing his new life, rather than doing traditional interviews with a sample of young fathers? Or what about choosing a couple of very different bars and spending three days in each to learn about the bar managers' relations to customers and staff? Should we use video cameras or not? Formal or informal interviews? There is a constant need to prioritize and think about which fieldwork strategies would work best. Similar processes can be found in academic projects, but they are often not brought out in the open in the same manner.

An important resource is the fact that several of the consultants and other professionals work closely in teams. This may in some ways compensate for the limited time. As part of a team you have to learn to forget the lone-wolf life of much academic research. Data, thoughts, and results must constantly be pooled and tested by others, and this means that new recruits from academia have to learn the techniques and skills of constantly sharing knowledge.

Another feature is the frequent use of contrastive or comparative international settings. Exploring the same problem in the French and the American hospital systems, or documenting how people organize family parties in five cities around the world, gives you a chance to avoid some of the bias of doing ethnography at home. Our point here is that tough budgeting, teamwork, and contrastive field sites may bring forward some new research skills that academia could certainly learn from.

THREE WAYS OF SURPRISING A CLIENT

A trend-analyst consultancy was hired by a large bank to investigate property bank loans among first-time buyers. When the projected finally kicked off after a year of talks with the potential client, the hired cultural analysts and the bank turned out to have very different views on the customers. The ethnographers wanted to understand how buying a house or an apartment was also buying a dream. It was necessary, therefore, to consider the emotional and irrational aspects of customers' economic behavior. How do people really accomplish a purchase of a property, was the basic question. The suggestion was to take on a number of general questions, such as: What is a home for you? What is your attitude to money and lending? What kinds of relations do property buyers develop with all the actors involved in a deal, especially the people in the bank? These questions gave the bank representatives quite new insights, since they usually thought in completely different ways.

After this, the ethnographers carried out fieldwork in seven households for three months. During that time, they kept up a close dialogue with the bank staff. At the conclusion of the project, they made a final presentation, partly by "telling stories" about their fieldwork experiences and about the hopes and fears, beliefs and dreams, of the bank customers. They also presented a written report about the facts and feelings related to the customers' investments, richly illustrated with pictures and quotes. It also contained concrete suggestions for solutions.

Doing such cultural translations may be a daunting task. A second example comes from a consultancy specializing in studying user-driven innovations. One of their projects was related to a medical manufacturer of bandages and tools for handling ostomies or incontinence conditions. The firm wanted to know if the ways they packaged and branded their products were really cost-effective. The consultants decided to use a classic ethnographic approach of "following the object" and observed how the products were dealt with by all kinds of groups, from the storage guys at the large hospitals, to doctors and nurses, and to very different kinds of patients. One of the methods used, for example, was the technique of "shadowing," closely following specialist nurses who dealt with newly diagnosed patients.

In order to obtain some contrastive material, the consultants decided to do fieldwork in French and American health-care systems. They made a video interview with an American male living without medical insurance in a trailer park who constantly struggled with the problems of affording bandages and his need to get back to work. This interview served as a very effective contrast to the French patients, who never had to worry about the cost or the length of their treatment. They also compared "veteran users," who had a history of handling their wounds, with people who were newly diagnosed and were having to adjust to a whole new life.

The insight the ethnographers brought back to the manufacturers was that the standard products they shipped around the world had very different meanings and uses in different situations. The needs of the people who handled these products were not really understood by the medical firm. By considering people's highly varying conditions and needs—their need for emotional support as well as directions for using the product, for example—the ethnographers succeeded in communicating a new, cultural perspective on this medical problem.

The third example regards a consultancy firm working with urban planning. They were approached by the local council of a working-class suburb in Copenhagen, a suburb dominated by grey high-rise buildings from the 1960s and endless rows of detached houses, and seen as devoid of any architectural beauty or interesting historical traditions. The council was brave enough to want to enter a competition for developing local heritage projects sponsored by the National Heritage Board and a large credit union. The ethnographic consultants were hired to make this unlikely project happen.

How do you identify, document, and communicate valuable traits of local heritage in a setting that is famous for having none? How do you find history in a community described as without history? In a limited period of time, a heritage plan was to be produced, a plan that resonated with different groups and subcultures in a community that included a wide variety of ethnic minorities as well as a social spectrum spanning from long-term working-class inhabitants to new middle-class commuters.

The consultants had to be really creative in trying to view this location with fresh eyes and explore what the locals valued and were attached to. In their fieldwork, they combined ethnographic methods such as "walk-and-talk" interviews and workshops with local people, bringing in reference groups for meetings in surprising settings, turning the inconspicuous or ignored into new assets. Instead of "freezing" interesting parts of the community defined as valuable heritage sites in the conventional ways, the analysts worked together with local actors to define themes that mirrored local practices. Typically, many of the detached houses had been built by working-class families, without any architectural guidance, and had been the objects of endless DIY projects of additions and rebuilding; it was precisely this individualism and constant improvisation that was singled out as a striking local tradition.

The final plan did work. To the astonishment of the fifty-three other competing communities and local councils, this Copenhagen suburb succeeded in being one of the four winners and was able to spend the next two years turning the new heritage ideas into practice. Again it was the surprise effect that made the job, seeing local conditions as potential and future landmarks that emphasized both some of the material and the mental infrastructures of local life.

These three cases outlined here shared a successful strategy of teaching the clients something they did not know and had not expected. To attain this effect, specific ethnographic strategies and tactics had to be developed. The consultants had to convince their clients that it was better to invest in qualitative and experimental methods than to just do "business as usual." Interestingly enough, all three projects could, albeit with different goals and organizational frameworks, also have been possible as "pure" academic projects.

SO WHAT?

One of the lessons that can be learned from applied cultural analysis is that in the world of business and public organizations you are always confronted with the question "So what?" All clients, regardless of their activity, want to know exactly what the cultural analysis will mean for their organization or company. They will not be satisfied by the answer that the world is complex and that it takes time to understand people and culture. They take for granted that the research results should have a real and immediate effect on what they are doing. "What do you suggest we should do?" is a question asked more rarely in academia.

Another lesson is that more interdisciplinary cooperation helps to counteract "a tunnel vision." In the medical device project, the researchers took advantage of collaborating with the designers in the medical firm, who were very good at practical solutions but were also sometimes trapped by their own creative thinking and initial sketches. The cultural analysts, on the other hand, were good at looking at the problems from unexpected angles but often got ensnared in the web of just criticizing what was wrong. However, together these two parties made a more effective team, ready to answer the tricky question "And now what?" We also hold the view that academia can learn from the applied-researchers' experiences of how to work fast and efficiently and how to utilize analytical perspectives in close cooperation with nonacademics. Working "out there" teaches you an ability to present your professional competence and findings convincingly and comprehensibly. It is absolutely necessary for the researchers' survival, in this market, to know how, for example, businesspeople and officials in various organizations think and speak and how they look upon academic research. This is knowledge that needs to be incorporated into university training in doing applied work.

THE CRITICAL EDGE

In the applied courses in which we have been involved, it is interesting to note what kinds of problems were voiced when the pros and cons of applied research were discussed. Sometimes the student groups were split in matters of how, when, why, and for whom one was ready to work. While some thought the critical edge of research would disappear or that ethics would be ignored, others felt that this was an "ivory tower" attitude, an excuse for not having to do the messy job of applying knowledge and following it being put to use. Such heated debates are important and may provoke self-reflection on both sides.

Both the students and the consultants were afraid their critical skills would not be appreciated in the world of business. Is this a real danger? It might be in some places. But, in fact, we see ethnography and cultural analysis as a substantially critical activity, wherever it is carried out. One of our points in this book is that cultural patterns tend to entrap people in a taken-for-granted reality. The role of the researcher will then be to question commonsense assumptions by describing and analyzing hidden agendas that inhibit, repress, and constrain people in their everyday lives. There is always a dimension of power in social life, but it is often found in surprising places and in unexpected forms.

Strikingly enough, it is precisely this critical perspective that the interviewees found most important in the academic baggage they carried with them into their new careers. This again underlines the importance of academic training for nurturing and developing critical thinking. Research that desperately tries to be "useful" or "easily applicable" may, in fact, end up becoming predictable or unchallenging if it loses its open, reflective, and critical perspective.

As our students returned from the field and their first applied jobs, they brought back not only important insights but also new skills and tools. They provided us with feedback on what was important in their earlier training and what could be improved. They had new experiences of teamwork and communicating with people to whom cultural analysis was an unknown field, and they developed skills for working under strong time pressures and making findings short, clear, and sharp. Most important, they learned to pick and use the tools in the analytical toolbox they had acquired at university. This is a comfort when suddenly finding yourself all alone with a camera on a cold morning in a nondescript suburb that is eagerly waiting to be documented.

REFERENCES

Amis, Kingsley. 1953. *Lucky Jim*. London: Gollancz.

Appadurai, Arjun. 1996. *Modernity at Large: Cultural Dimensions of Modernity*. Minneapolis: University of Minnesota Press.

Arnold, Jeanne E., et al. 2012. *Life at Home in the Twenty-First Century: Thirty-Two Families Open Their Doors*. Los Angeles: Cotzen Institute of Archeology Press.

Böhme, Gernot. 2006. *Architektur und Atmosphäre*. München: Wilhelm Fink Verlag.

Brennan, Teresa. 2004. *The Transmission of Affect*. New York: Cornell University Press.

Cahir, Jayde, and Ann Werner. 2013. "Escaping the Everyday: Young People's Use of Text Messages and Songs." *Youth Studies Australia* 32 (2).

Chang, Heewon. 2008. *Autoethnography as Method*. Walnut Creek, CA: Left Coast Press.

Church, Kate, Jenny Weight, Marsha Berry, and Hugh Macdonald. 2010. "At Home with Media Technology." *Home Cultures* 7 (3): 263–86.

Clifford, James, and George Marcus, eds. 1986. *Writing Culture: The Poetics and Politics of Ethnography*. Berkeley: University of California Press.

Darrah, Charles N., James M. Freeman, and J. A. English-Lueck. 2007. *Busier than Ever! Why American Families Can't Slow Down*. Stanford, CA: Stanford University Press.

Deleuze, Gilles, and Félix Guattari. 1987. *A Thousand Plateaus: Capitalism and Schizophrenia*. Minneapolis: University of Minnesota Press.

Denny, Rita, and Patricia L. Sutherland, eds. 2014. *Handbook of Anthropology of Business*. Walnut Creek, CA: Left Coast Press.

Denzin, Norman. 1997. *Interpretive Ethnography: Ethnographic Practices for the Twenty-First Century*. London: Sage.

Douglas, Mary. 1991. "The Idea of Home: A Kind of Space." *Social Research* 58 (1): 288–307.

Ehn, Billy, and Orvar Löfgren. 2010. *The Secret World of Doing Nothing*. Berkeley: University of California Press.

Ellis, Carolyn. 2004. *The Ethnographic I: A Methodological Novel about Autoethnography*. Walnut Creek, CA: AltaMira Press.

Fiske, John. 1990. *Introduction to Communication Studies*. London: Routledge.

Fornäs, Johan. 2013. "Mediated Identity Formation: Current Trends in Research and Society." *New Media, New Research Challenges* 20 (2).

Frykman, Jonas. 1990. "What People Do, but Seldom Say." *Ethnologia Scandinavica* 20: 50–62.

Garvey, Pauline. 2001. "Organized Disorder: Moving Furniture in Norwegian Homes." In *Home Possessions: The Material Culture of the Home*, edited by Daniel Miller. Berg: Oxford.

Gauntlett, David. 2011. *Making Is Connecting: The Social Meaning of Creativity, from DIY and Knitting to YouTube and Web 2.0*. Cambridge: Polity.

Geertz, Clifford. 1967. "Under the Mosquito Net." *The New York Review of Books*, September 14.

Gillis, John. 1996. *A World of Their Own Making: Myth, Ritual, and the Quest for Family Values*. New York: Basic Books.

Goffman, Erving. 1959/1990. *Presentation of Self in Everyday Life*. London: Penguin.

———. 1967/2005. *Interaction Ritual: Essays in Face-to-Face Behavior*. New Brunswick, NJ: Aldine Transaction.

Goodall, H. L. 2000. *Writing the New Ethnography*. Oxford: Altamira Press.

Göess, Mareike Sibilla. 2011. "Going Native with the Digital: Practices, Values, and Innovation in the Information Age." MA thesis in Applied Cultural Analysis, Lund University.

Hall, E. T. 1959. *The Silent Language*. New York: Doubleday.

Haraway, Donna. 1991. *Simians, Cyborgs, and Women: The Reinvention of Nature*. New York: Routledge.

Harper, Douglas. 1987. *Working Knowledge: Skill and Community in a Small Shop*. Berkeley: University of California Press.

Henriques, Julian. 2010. "The Vibrations of Affect and Their Propagation on a Night Out on Kingston's Dancehall Scene." *Body & Society* 16 (1): 57–89.

Hiss, Tony. 1991. *The Experience of Place: A Completely New Way of Looking at and Dealing with Our Radically Changing Cities and Countryside*. New York: Alfred Knopf.

Hoechsmann, Michael, and Stuart R. Poyntz. 2012. *Media Literacies: A Critical Introduction*. Hoboken, NJ: Wiley-Blackwell.

Illouz, Eva. 2007. *Cold Intimacies: The Making of Emotional Capitalism*. Cambridge: Polity Press.

Ingold, Tim. 2011. *Being Alive: Essays on Movement, Knowledge and Description*. Abingdon, Oxon: Routledge.

Kaufmann, Jean-Claude. 2002. *Premier matin: Comment naît une histoire d'amour*. Paris: Armand Colin.

Kjær, Sarah Holst. 2009. *Sådan er det at elske: En kulturanalyse af parforhold*. København: Museum Tusculanum.

Kopytoff, Igor. 1986. "The Cultural Biography of Things: Commoditization as a Process." In *The Social Life of Things: Commodities in a Cultural Perspective*, edited by Arjun Appadurai. Cambridge: Cambridge University Press.

Körber, Karin. 2012. "So Far and Yet So Near: Present-Day Transnational Families." *Ethnologia Europaea* 42 (2): 12–25.

Kusserow, Adrie. 2004. *American Individualisms: Child Rearing and Social Class in Three Neighborhoods*. New York: Palgrave Macmillan.

Light, Andrew, and Jonathan M. Smith, eds. 2005. *The Aesthetics of Everyday Life*. New York: Columbia University Press.

Linde-Laursen, Anders. 1993. "The Nationalization of Trivialities: How Cleaning Becomes an Identity Marker in the Encounter of Swedes and Danes." *Ethnos* 58 (3–4): 275–93.

Littlefield, Carla N., and Emilia Gonzalez-Clements. 2008. "Creating Your Own Consulting Business." *NAPA Bulletin* 29: 152–65.

Marvin, Carolyn. 1988. *When Old Technologies Were New: Thinking about Electric Communication in the Late Nineteenth Century*. New York: Oxford University Press.

Massey, Doreen. 2005. *For Space*. London: Sage.

Maushart, Susan. 2010. *The Winter of Our Disconnect*. London: Profile.

Miller, Daniel. 2001. *Home Possessions: Material Culture behind Closed Doors*. Oxford: Berg.

———. 2008. *The Comfort of Things*. Oxford: Blackwell.

Nielsen, Louise. 2012. "Emotions on the Move: Mobile Emotions among Train Commuters in the South East of Denmark." *Emotion, Space and Society* 5 (3): 201–6.

Nippert-Eng, Christina. 2010. *Islands of Privacy*. Chicago: Chicago University Press.

Orlikowski, Wanda J. 2012. "Sociomaterial Practices: Exploring Technology at Work." *Organization Studies* 28 (9): 1435–48.

Parks, Lisa. 2006. "Falling Apart: Electronics Salvaging and the Global Media Economy." In *Residual Media*, edited by Charles R. Acland. Minneapolis: University of Minnesota Press.

Pink, Sarah. 2004. *Home Truths: Gender, Domestic Objects and Everyday Life*. Oxford: Berg.

———. 2007. *Doing Visual Ethnography: Images, Media and Representation in Research*. London: Sage.

———. 2009. *Doing Sensory Ethnography*. London: Sage.

Prensky, Marc. 2001. "Digital Natives, Digital Immigrants." *On the Horizon* 9 (1): 1–6.

Queneau, Raymond. 1947/1979. *Exercises in Style*. London: John Calder.

Shove, Elizabeth, Matthew Watson, Martin Hand, and Jack Ingram. 2007. *The Design of Everyday Life*. New York: Berg.

Shove, Elizabeth, Mika Pantzar, and Matthew Watson. 2012. *The Dynamics of Social Practice: Everyday Life and How It Changes*. Thousand Oaks, CA: Sage.

Silverstone, Roger, and Eric Hirsch. 1992. *Consuming Technologies: Media and Information in Domestic Spaces*. London: Routledge.

Simmel, Georg. 1910. "How Is Society Possible?" *American Journal of Sociology* 16.

Smith, Patti. 2009. *Just Kids: From Brooklyn to the Chelsea Hotel—a Life of Art and Friendship*. New York: Ecco Press.

Sønderby, Knud. 1931. *Midt i en Jazztid*. København: Gyldendal.

Straw, Laura. 2008. "The Art and Craft of Train Travel." *Social and Cultural Geography* 9 (6): 711–26.

Svensson, Julia. 2010. "Spår med snår." *Sydsvenska Dagbladet* 4 (February): B4.

Tan, Qian Hui. 2012. "Smell in the City: Smoking and Olfactory Politics." *Urban Studies*, September 18.

Trovalla, Ulrika, and Erik Trovalla. 2015. "Infrastructure Turned Suprastructure: Unpredictable Materialities and Visions of a Nigerian Nation." *Journal of Material Culture* March 20(1): 43–57.

Vannini, Phillip. 2012. *Ferry Tales: Mobility, Place, and Time on Canada's West Coast.* London: Routledge.

———. ed. 2015. *Non-representational Theory and Methodologies: Re-envisioning Research.* London: Routledge.

Verrips, Jojada. 1994. "The Thing Didn't 'Do' What I Wanted: Some Notes on Modern Animism in Western Societies." In *Transactions: Essays in Honour of Jeremy F. Boissevain,* edited by Jojada Verrips. Amsterdam: Het Spinhuis.

Wallendorf, Melanie, and Eric J. Arnould. 1991. "'We Gather Together': The Consumption Rituals of Thanksgiving Day." *Journal of Consumer Research* 18 (13): 6–31.

Warneken, Bernd Jürgen, et al., eds. 1998. *Das Outfit der Wissenschaft: Zur symbolischer Represäntation akademischer Fächer.* Tübingen: Tübinger Vereinigung für Volkskunde.

Werner, Ann. 2012. "Emotions in Music Culture: The Circulation of Love." *Global Media Journal: Australian Edition* 6 (1), http://www.commarts.uws.edu.au/gm jau/v6_2012_1/ann_werner_RA.html.

Wilk, Richard. 2005. "Smoothing." *Ethnologia Europaea* 35 (1–2).

Winther, Ida Wentzel. 2006. *Hjemlighed: Kulturfænomenologiske studier.* København: Danmarks Pædagogiske Universitets Forlag.

Wolf, Margery. 1992. *A Thrice-Told Tale. Feminism, Postmodernism, and Ethnographic Responsibility.* Stanford: Stanford University Press.

INDEX

ABOUT THE AUTHORS

Billy Ehn is professor emeritus of ethnology at Umeå University in Sweden. He is coauthor, with Orvar Löfgren, of *The Secret World of Doing Nothing*.

Orvar Löfgren is professor emeritus of ethnology at Lund University. His publications include *On Holiday: A History of Vacationing*.

Richard Wilk is Provost's Professor of Anthropology at Indiana University. His publications include *Fast Food/Slow Food* and *Economies and Cultures* (second edition, with Lisa Cliggett). Richard Wilk and Orvar Löfgren, together with Jessica Chelakis, are coeditors of The Anthropology of Everyday Life, a Rowman & Littlefield series.